Top row left to right: Howard Carter, Smith Wigglesworth
Bottom row left to right: Mark Buntain, Lester Sumrall, R.W. Schambach

Unless otherwise indicated, all Scripture quotations are from the King James Version of the Bible.

Good, Better, Best: The Gift of Faith
ISBN 978-1-7336042-8-4

Copyright © 2023 by Ted Shuttlesworth Evangelistic Association, Inc.

All rights reserved. Content and/or cover may not be reproduced in whole or in part or in any form without the express written consent of the publisher.

www.tedshuttlesworth.com

Published by T.S.E.A., Inc.
Post Office Box 7
Farmington, West Virginia 26571
USA

Cover design by Ted Shuttlesworth Jr.

Printed in the United States of America

Howard Carter exhorts on the importance of the gift of faith

"Yes; the gift of faith is the greatest manifestation of the three gifts of power, faith, versus the working of miracles and gifts of healing. It definitely calls into operation the powers of the world to come, uniting angels with men for the accomplishment of the Divine purpose."

Questions and Answers on the Gifts of the Spirit, Harrison House, Tulsa, OK, 1976, p. 52.

CONTENTS

Foreword	vii
Introduction	xi
1. Good, Better, Best	1
2. What is the Gift of Faith?	29
3. The Four Kinds of Bible Faith	45
4. Courage in the Time of Crisis	57
5. Living in the Overflow	81
6. An Instrument of Dominion	113
7. Questions and Answers	157

Foreword

This book, *"Good, Better, Best"* by Evangelist Ted Shuttlesworth Sr. focuses on the gift of faith. I have known him since April, 1989. I met him in the second year of my ministry in the United States of America, when I was ministering at Zion Bible Institute, in Barrington, Rhode Island.

In one of the meetings that week, he was sitting on the platform, and I turned to him and said these words, "The Lord told me to tell you that you will travel." Several of the instructors laughed, because he was already traveling as an evangelist.

What they did not know was he had just returned from London, England, where he had been offered a church to pastor.

The Word from the Lord that I gave him was a confirmation that he was to continue doing what he was doing. We subsequently became good friends.

One of the things that I appreciate most about his life is that he has always been consistent and true to himself. He stayed faithful to the calling and assignment that God has given him.

He unwaveringly kept his commitment to preach the Gospel with power, signs, wonders, and miracles. It spoke volumes to me that he sacrificed his own ministry for ten years to help and serve Evangelist R. W. Schambach.

We have run parallel in many areas of ministry over the years, and he and I track in the Spirit together. I know that when I hear from the Lord on a particular issue, the Lord will be speaking the exact same or similar things to him.

He has been a great encouragement to me and to my wife, Adonica, and he has been a great blessing to our church, The River at Tampa Bay, every time he has ministered there.

This book will encourage you to *"covet earnestly"* the best gifts (of the Spirit) as the Lord directs us to do; which of course would be the one you need at the time. He has found the gift of faith is the best one for him, because it opens the door to the rest of the supernatural realm. This has definitely been the case in our ministry as well.

I believe this book will lift your faith and create a hunger in you to go after all that has been made available to you by the power of the Holy Spirit.

Dr. Rodney Howard-Browne
Revival Ministries International
Tampa, Florida, USA
April 2023

Introduction

The gifts of the Spirit and their use have consumed my life since my early boyhood. My father consistently taught about the gifts, especially in the midweek services in the churches he pastored. My parents taught me and my brothers about the Holy Spirit. We were instructed not to grieve the Spirit by our words and deeds. He was the unseen person that watched over us.

My early memories are filled with the demonstrations of the Spirit in the services. There were tongues and interpretations, healings, visible miracles, words of revelation, and a spirit of faith that filled the atmosphere. It produced a spirit of expectancy that helped us to *receive* from the Lord.

There was a library of books in our home that were

faith-building. They inspired me to know more about the Lord and the working of the Holy Spirit. The authors were men and women of God that worked in the supernatural anointing of the Spirit.

My father knew I liked adventure. He gave me books about missionaries like George Mueller and Victor Plymire. Lester Sumrall's *"The Invisible Boy"* stirred my imagination about the power of God. These books gave me a desire to read about the exploits of men and women of faith. I read my Bible differently as I began to study the things of the Spirit.

My personal library has become a treasure trove of books on the gifts of the Spirit. One of these books was by Howard Carter. He pioneered the teaching of the gifts of the Spirit that influenced many in the Voice of Healing movement after World War II.

Lester Sumrall traveled with him around the world, learning how to operate in and demonstrate these wonderful gifts. Dr. Sumrall wrote concerning Howard Carter's first time operating in the gift of faith:

> It was during World War I while Brother Carter was jailed as a conscientious objector. His cell was small, uncomfortable, and damp. Overhead, water dripped on him incessantly, almost driving him mad. Looking up toward the ceiling, he said,

"I command you water to flow the other way."
Immediately the water ceased to fall.[1]

So it was during the First World War that he began his study on the gifts of the Spirit. The Lord came to him in that prison cell and revealed to him how these gifts operated and what they were. Later, Brother Carter founded England's first Pentecostal Bible school, Hampstead Bible School, in London.

I had the privilege of being with Dr. Sumrall in the early days of my ministry. His stories were inspiring, and his faith was contagious. He allowed me to preach in his church in South Bend, on Ireland Road, and do television with him, as well as preach on his radio network with his son Frank.

When I left South Bend, my wife and I traveled to Illinois. It was a windy day in Chicago, and there is nothing unusual about that, but the minister walking with us on LaSalle turned and gave us an unusual prophecy.

"Someday, you will minister with the preachers and leaders of today. I see you will preach under a tent with R. W. Schambach; you will meet Kenneth Hagin

---

1. Sumrall, Lester, *Weapons of Our Warfare*, Lester Sumrall Evangelistic Association, Inc. 1965. Print.

and T. L. Osborn. You will be used by God in the gifts." My wife and I hid that divine moment in our hearts for several years, and then that word began to come to pass.

Later, the Lord allowed us to travel, preach, and eat with and fellowship with many of his dear servants. We were blessed to spend time with Brothers Sumrall, Hagin, Schambach, John Osteen, T.L. Osborn, Dave Nunn and James Dunn, Sister Lindsay, Morris Cerullo, and Oral Roberts, to name a few.

There were hundreds of faithful pastors who gave us their wise counsel and help. All of these anointed servants of God told us their stories and gave advice, and we are a product of their faithfulness.

Pentecostal denominational lines are being blurred, and I see a coming together of hungry young men and women who desire a genuine move of God, nothing more and nothing less.

Our world demands proof. Fact-checkers have replaced science and are molding their own humanistic religion, which is nothing more than godless socialism and atheistic communism repackaged to deceive the people.

The gifts of the Spirit are needed now more than ever to deal with the end-time deception that the Bible warns us about. *"But evil men and seducers shall wax worse and worse, deceiving, and being deceived."* (2 Timothy 3:13)

We know that before Jesus returns, there will be two parallel moves in the spirit realm. There will be a tremendous outpouring of the Holy Spirit upon the earth. He will move for the world in great power to redeem and bless those who will receive him.

> **And it shall come to pass afterward, that I will pour out my spirit upon all flesh; and your sons and your daughters shall prophesy, your old men shall dream dreams, your young men shall see visions: And also upon the servants and upon the handmaids in those days will I pour out my spirit.**
>
> **Joel 2:28, 29**

Peter stood up on the Day of Pentecost and confirmed that the outpouring of the Holy Spirit and the 120 believers who were filled with the Spirit and spoke in other tongues was the fulfillment of this prophecy given by Joel. Peter said, *"But this is that which was spoken by the prophet Joel;"* (Acts 2:16)

The Spirit of God, we are told, shall come as the former and latter rains. (Joel 2:23) The Former rain was the planting rain that prepared the ground for the seed. The Latter rain was for the harvest and the time of reaping.

Simultaneously, the Scripture records, there will come an invasion from hell! Demonic activity will increase as we draw closer to the coming of Christ.

> **Therefore rejoice ye heavens, and ye that dwell in them. Woe to the inhabiters of the earth and of the sea! For the devil is come down unto you, having great wrath, because he knoweth that he hath but a short time.**
>
> **Revelation 12:12**

The outpouring of the Spirit will come upon our sons and daughters. Our children will receive the mighty baptism of the Holy Spirit! However, the devil will also target the children for deception and destruction.

It is in this time of crisis that the gift of faith is needed. The Holy Spirit comes bearing gifts like Eliezer of old. Abraham enlisted the help of his servant Eliezer to go and bring back a bride for his son.

> And the servant took ten camels of the camels of his master, and departed; for all THE GOODS of his master were in his hand: and he arose, and went to Mesopotamia, unto the city of Nahor.
> **Genesis 24:10**

Eliezer represents the Holy Spirit. When he climbed upon his camel and brought with him the string of nine other camels, it would speak to us of the Holy Spirit and the nine gifts of the Spirit God the Father has sent. Rebekah is the type of the Church, the bride for God's Son.

We need to understand that it takes the gifts of the Holy Spirit to separate the Church from the world, and it takes the same gifts to bring the Church back to the Father in Heaven.

The gift of faith is one of these nine gifts of the Spirit, which will grow stronger in operation because of the end-time danger:

> This know also, that in the last days PERILOUS TIMES shall come.
> **2 Timothy 3:1**

It is in this last-day time of great crises that we need to seek the Lord for a mighty move of his Spirit. Lord, send us your faithful servant, the Holy Spirit! When Satan rages, we cannot be defeated. God's mighty power and the weapons of our warfare (Ephesians 5:18), guarantee us a victorious conclusion.

I believe that it is time to challenge a new generation to seek after the Lord. These are my notes and messages from over forty-seven years of my quest to, *"desire spiritual gifts"* (1 Corinthians 14:1).

Ted Shuttlesworth
Hill Cottage, WV
February 2023

CHAPTER 1

Good, Better, Best

But covet earnestly the BEST gifts: and yet shew I unto you a more excellent way.
1 Corinthians 12:31

There is a good, there is a better, but God has a best, a higher standard for us than we have yet attained. It is a better thing if it is God's plan and not ours.
– Smith Wigglesworth

God's plan is for us to excel in the things of the Spirit. The world needs to see less of us and more of God. "Sir, we would see Jesus." (John 12:21). Only the Lord can set a sinful soul free. He and only he can bring healing to the sick and diseased. A desperate world demands a dynamic answer. Christ is the Answer!

The Apostle Paul challenges us to *"covet earnestly the best gifts."* Therefore we begin to understand that some gifts are better than others; however, this does not diminish any gift because all the gifts *"profit withal"* (1 Corinthians 12:7).

The Apostle Paul lists the nine gifts of the Spirit.

> **For to one is given by the Spirit the WORD OF WISDOM; to another the WORD OF KNOWLEDGE by the same Spirit; to another FAITH by the same Spirit; to another the GIFTS OF HEALING by the same Spirit; to another THE WORKING OF MIRACLES; to another PROPHECY; to another DISCERNING OF SPIRITS; to another DIVERS KINDS OF TONGUES; to another THE INTERPRETATION OF TONGUES:**
>
> **1 Corinthians 12:8-10**

These gifts all have differences in *administration* and in *operations* (1 Corinthians 12:5, 6). Each gift is unique to its own purpose, and they work as the Spirit wills. *"But all these worketh that one and the selfsame Spirit, dividing to every man SEVERALLY as he will."* (1 Corinthians 12:11)

These are not the skills or abilities of man. The *word of wisdom* is not received by studying at a university. *Tongues* are not derived from studying linguistics in a language sound lab. These are supernatural gifts and so much so that:

> **Now when they saw the boldness of Peter and John, and perceived that THEY WERE UNLEARNED and IGNORANT MEN, they marvelled; and they took knowledge of them, that they had been with Jesus.**
>
> **Acts 4:13**

A believer can operate in several gifts and may become more proficient in certain gifts. There are some who have great faith in getting the deaf healed but not in other notable miracles, such as the blind or the crippled. One minister that I saw had a powerful gift that dealt with tumors and goiters. Yet he did not see very many blind people healed.

CHRIST HEALED THE BLIND IN TRINIDAD

There was a minister in Trinidad that saw scores of blind healed in his ministry. He started a church and called it *Jesus Heals the Blind Church*. I preached there in the late 1980s, and the first miracle that took place was when I prayed for a blind woman, and she received her sight! There seemed to be a breakthrough in that church for that, and the Spirit used me though I had not seen very many healed of blindness at that time.

Then certain gifts are given to each of the five-fold ministry gifts to help them in their ministry (Ephesians 4:11). Pastors and teachers may have *discerning of spirits, gifts of healing, prophecy,* and may be used in the others. Evangelists should have the *working of miracles, word of knowledge, and gifts of healing.* A prophet may have the *word of knowledge and wisdom, prophecy, working of miracles, and tongues and interpretation* as the Spirit uses this office.

PAUL REPRESENTS THE OFFICE OF AN APOSTLE

Paul ministered with the *word of wisdom.*

> **And saw him saying unto me, Make haste, and GET THEE QUICKLY OUT OF JERUSALEM: for they will not receive thy testimony concerning me.**
> **Acts 22:18**

Paul was praying in the temple in Jerusalem when he fell into a trance *(a suspended state)*. He saw the Lord and was given instructions concerning what to do. This is a classic example of the word of wisdom.

Paul received a *word of knowledge.*

> **The same heard Paul speak: who stedfastly beholding him, and PERCEIVING that he had faith to be healed,**
>
> **Acts 14:9**

Paul "perceived" that this young man had faith for his miracle. That is the revelation gift of the *word of knowledge.* He was born a cripple and heard the Gospel for the first time. He received faith when he found out that Jesus heals the crippled. The *word of knowledge* reveals information in the present and also the past. Then by the *working of miracles,* the young man was healed. Two gifts worked together to bring about this great work of Christ.

Paul received the *gift of faith.*

> **And God wrought special miracles by the hands of Paul: So that from his body were brought unto the sick handkerchiefs or aprons, and the diseases de-**

> parted from them, and the evil spirits went out of them.
>
> Acts 19:11, 12

The *gift of faith,* or special faith, produces wonder-working power. How did Paul know to wear these cloths on his body? The handkerchiefs and aprons became a "point of contact" for the sick, yet Paul had laid his hands on the cloths *before* the sick received them. He received the special faith that produced special miracles. (Read the chapter on Questions and Answers about the Gift of Faith.)

Paul was used in the *gifts of healing.*

> And it came to pass, that the father of Publius lay sick of a fever and of a bloody flux: to whom Paul entered in, and prayed, and laid his hands on him, AND HEALED HIM So when this was done, others also, which had diseases in the island, came, AND WERE HEALED.
>
> Acts 28:8, 9

Paul did what every believer may do; he laid his hands on the sick. You, too, can minister to the sick by the laying on of hands. Jesus taught, *"They shall take up serpents; and if they drink any deadly thing, it shall not hurt them; THEY SHALL LAY HANDS ON THE SICK, and they shall recover."* (Mark 16:18)

One of the ways that the gifts of healing may be administered is by the laying on of hands. Paul released these gifts of healing by laying his hands on Publius's father, which brought healing to him as well as others who were diseased on the island, and they were healed, too (Acts 28:8, 9).

Paul operated in the *working of miracles.*

> **The same heard Paul speak: who stedfastly beholding him, and perceiving that he had faith to be healed, Said with a loud voice, Stand upright on thy feet. And he leaped and walked.**
>
> **Acts 14:9, 10**

The Bible declares that this young man was crippled from birth. He had never walked. Paul comes into his town, and we read, *"And there they preached the Gospel."* (Acts 14:7). We know that this was the first time the Gospel had ever been preached in Lystra and Derbe. Since the young man received, faith for his miracle and faith comes from hearing the Word (Romans 10:17), then miracles are a part of the Gospel message.

> **Through mighty SIGNS AND WONDERS, by the power of the Spirit of God; so that from Jerusalem, and round about unto Illyricum, I have fully preached THE GOSPEL OF CHRIST.**
>
> **Romans 15:19**

Miracles confirmed the Gospel then and miracles confirm the Gospel NOW!

Paul was used in the *gift of prophecy.*

> **And now I exhort you to be of good cheer: for THERE SHALL BE NO LOSS OF ANY MAN'S LIFE among you, but of the ship.**
>
> **Acts 27:22**

Exhortation is a part of the gift of prophecy, and I am sure that this word brought comfort or peace to the crew and soldiers that day. I like the thought that after prayer and fasting, Paul gave this word of prophecy. *"And now I exhort you to be of good cheer: for there shall be no loss of any man's life among you, but of the ship"* (Acts 27:22).

I believe that he received the *gift of faith* from the Spirit when the angel spoke to him. Praise God for his goodness to watch over us.

Paul had *discerning of spirits.*

> **And it came to pass, as we went to prayer, a certain damsel possessed with A SPIRIT OF DIVINATION met us, which brought her masters much gain by soothsaying: The same followed Paul and us, and cried, saying, These men are the servants of the most high God, which shew unto us the way of salvation. And this did she many days. But Paul, being grieved, turned and SAID TO THE SPIRIT I command thee in the name of Jesus Christ to come out of her. And he came out the same hour.**
>
> **Acts 16:16-18**

Paul rebuked the spirit of divination in the woman after *"many days."* It would seem at first that the woman was simply encouraging the people that Paul and Silas were men of God whose message would bring salvation.

The time came when Paul felt grieved in his spirit about the woman, and at that moment, he turned and commanded the spirit to come out. All the gifts work at the moment or at the time that they are needed. *Discerning of spirits* is an important gift in the casting out of devils.

Paul spoke in tongues.

> **I thank my God, I speak with tongues more than ye all:**
> **1 Corinthians 14:18**

He also encouraged the early Church that they were to pray for the interpretation of tongues so that the Church would be blessed. *"Wherefore let him that speaketh in an unknown tongue pray that he may interpret."* (1 Corinthians 14:13)

Since Paul said that he spoke in *"tongues"* more than those in the Corinthian church and instructed them to pray for interpretation, then he must have interpreted them as well.

We see that Paul stood in the office of the apostle and that he was used by the Holy Spirit in all the nine gifts. *However, any believer filled with the Spirit may expect to be used in any of the nine gifts when they are needed.*

THE BEST GIFT IS THE ONE THAT IS NEEDED

We were holding a tent meeting at the fairgrounds in Terre Haute, Indiana. The meetings would begin on a Friday night and then go on for ten days. It was the opening weekend, and the Lord was moving, and several deaf people were healed. A couple came to me and asked me if I would pray for their brother if they brought him from the deaf school. They could get him out on Sunday. I encouraged them to bring him.

That Sunday afternoon, they came and brought the deaf brother with them. There are several messages that I preach that produce an atmosphere for miracles. If you preach salvation, people should get saved. If you preach about receiving the mighty baptism of the Spirit, people should be filled with the Holy Ghost. When you preach on the working of miracles, then miracles take place. *You get what you preach!*

When I was done preaching, I invited everyone down to the altar who needed a miracle. One of the things that I do is demonstrate God's power before I give an altar call for salvation. I learned to do this in India in 1981. A minister, one C. Zechariah, challenged me when I was preaching there to invite people to Christ *after* demonstrating the gifts of healing and the working of miracles.

My answer to him was, "But that would take faith." Looking back, I laugh at the inexperience of my youth, but many times now, I demonstrate even before I preach. It prepares the hearts to receive.

That hot summer day in Indiana, I felt to pray for miracles before I gave the altar call. We had quite a few folks that had come out who were not saved. The ministry of Jesus is always our example. *"Many believed in his name, when they saw the miracles which he did."* (John 2:23)

I introduced the crowd to the couple that had brought their brother from the Indiana deaf school. They told the people he had been deaf since birth and could not talk. When I went to lay my hands on him to pray, suddenly, a woman down on one end of the altar began to speak loudly in tongues.

The only way I could describe it was it felt like cold water in my face. I was taken back and did not know why I felt grieved in my spirit, but I did. So I spoke to that woman to hold the message in tongues for later. She got mad and began to speak even louder in tongues. Out of my spirit, these words came, "That is not the gift needed now, but we need the working of miracles."

Well, she stomped out of the tent. When she did, a wonderful presence of God came under that tent! I commanded the deaf spirits to come out of the boy's ears, and they did! The crowd began to rejoice, and the boy grinned from ear to ear. Praise God forevermore!

I believe every sinner was saved that day. When the meeting was done, and my wife and I were driving out of town, we saw the boy standing in front of the grocery store drinking an orange soda. I said to my wife, "Watch this". . . honking the horn, we watched him turn his head and wave to us. That is how you want to leave a meeting.

The best gift is the one that is needed at the time. I learned this firsthand in Indiana; it was not *tongues* but the *working of miracles* that was needed. That day it was the BEST GIFT.

THE BEST UTTERANCE GIFT

The gifts of the Spirit fall beautifully into three distinct categories. Paul taught, *"Now there are diversities of gifts, but the same Spirit."* (1 Corinthians 12:4). Their divisions are determined by the nature of the gift in connection to their operation.

Three of the gifts help us to *speak* like God. Some refer to these as the utterance gifts or vocal gifts. They are *tongues, the interpretation of tongues, and prophecy.* The Scripture indicates that prophecy is the greatest of the *utterance gifts.*

> **Follow after charity, and desire spiritual gifts, but rather that ye may PROPHESY.**
>
> **1 Corinthians 14:1**

The apostle Paul encouraged believers to use these *utterance gifts* with the goal of the building up and blessing of the Church. When you speak in an unknown tongue, you are talking to God; but no one else understands you. (1 Corinthians 14:2)

When you prophesy, you bless all who hear it. Prophecy is given in the language of the people where you are. Prophecy is greater than the gift of tongues. *"For greater is he THAT PROPHESIETH than he that SPEAKETH WITH TONGUES, except he interpret,"* (1 Corinthians 14:5)

Then by operation, tongues are lesser than the gift of prophecy. Tongues with the interpretation can bless the hearers, yet they are only *equal* to prophecy. Thus prophecy is greater than both of these two, making prophecy the greatest of the *utterance gifts.*

Prophecy is the BEST of the *utterance gifts* also because it brings the lost to repentance and full surrender to the Lord: *"But IF ALL PROPHESY, and there come in* one that believeth not, or one unlearned, he is convinced of all, he is judged of all: and thus are the secrets of his heart made manifest; and so falling down on his face HE WILL WORSHIP GOD, and report that God is in you of a truth."* (1 Corinthians 14:24, 25)

THE BEST REVELATION GIFT

Three of the gifts help us to *think* like God. They are the *word of wisdom, the word of knowledge, and the discerning of spirits.* Their operation is by the Spirit giving us a fragment of information from the great reservoir of God's mind and purpose. You never receive it all, but rather, *"For now we see through a glass, darkly; but then face to face: NOW I KNOW IN PART; but then shall I know even as also I am known."* (1 Corinthians 13:12)

The *word of wisdom* reveals some future event that may affect an individual to bring about the best possible conclusion and result for that believer. It always speaks to the future.

The *word of knowledge* is a fragment of information from the mind of God concerning people, places, and things or conditions that affect a person. It reveals all these things from the past and even the present.

Discerning of spirits is seen in operation in the first chapter of the Gospel of John. It functions in all of the three realms of time: past, present, and future. John the Baptist discerned that Christ was the Lamb of God when he saw him at the Jordan River (John 1:29). When Nathanael stood in front of Jesus, the Lord saw that in the present, Nathanael was a man in whom was no guile. He also knew that in the past, Nathanael had been standing under a fig tree. Then the Lord showed how this gift reveals the future when he said, *"And he saith unto him, Verily, verily, I say unto you, Hereafter ye shall see heaven open, and the angels of God ascending and descending upon the Son of man."* (John 1:51)

The *word of wisdom* is for the future, and the *word of knowledge* is for the past and present, but the *discerning of spirits* has the greater operation of the three *revelation gifts* in that it touches the past, present, and future. That makes the *discerning of spirits* the BEST of the *revelation gifts*.

THE BEST POWER GIFT

Three of the gifts help us to *act* like God. They are *faith, the working of miracles, and the gift of healing*. Again the best gift is the one needed at the moment. That is what determines how we minister to the one that Lord has given us to bless. We refer to these gifts as the *power gifts*.

First, we need to look at the difference between the *working of miracles and the gift of healing.* Miracles are instantaneous, whereas the gift of healing is progressive. What is a miracle? *A miracle is a demonstration of the power of God that is a supernatural intervention over the laws of nature by the Holy Spirit.* The *working of miracles* is the third power gift listed in (1 Corinthians 12:10).

We could say that the *working of miracles shows the power of God and that the gifts of healing reveal the love and compassion of God.*

> **And Jesus went forth, and saw a great multitude, and was moved with COMPASSION toward them, and he HEALED their sick.**
> **Matthew 14:14**

Another difference between the working of miracles and the gifts of healing is revealed in their order of operation. Paul taught, *"And God hath set some in the church, first apostles, secondarily prophets, thirdly teachers, AFTER THAT MIRACLES, THEN GIFTS OF HEALINGS, helps, governments, diversities of tongues.* (1 Corinthians 12:28) Notice; gifts of healings are listed after miracles.

Mark's Gospel is considered to be the "miracle book"

of the four Gospels. The keywords that are descriptive of the working of miracles in this Gospel are forthwith, immediately, and straightway.

When Jesus turned the water into wine, that was a miracle, *"This beginning of MIRACLES did Jesus in Cana of Galilee, and manifested forth his glory; and his disciples believed on him."* (John 2:11). A miracle manifests by the Holy Spirit instantly.

Healing is different in that it takes place over a period of time to reach its conclusion.

> **And as he was now going down, his servants met him, and told him, saying, Thy son liveth. Then enquired he of them THE HOUR WHEN HE BEGAN TO AMEND. And they said unto him, YESTERDAY at the seventh hour the fever left him. So the father knew that it was at the same hour, in the which Jesus said unto him, Thy son liveth: and himself believed, and his whole house.**
> **John 4:51-53**

Recovery is a process of getting well.

When I was in Chicago at the University auditorium, I prayed for a woman named Esther who had cancerous tumors in her neck. I took a bottle of water and had the crowd stand, and we prayed the Scripture; *"And ye shall serve the Lord your God, and he shall bless thy bread, and thy water; and I will take sickness away from the midst of thee."* (Exodus 23:25) instantly those tumors disappeared from her neck! God used the working of miracles to accomplish it!

The tent was up in Miami, Florida. A young woman from the Middle East named Shabaz came, and when she stood in front of me, the word of knowledge revealed that she had cancerous tumors. I laid hands on her and prayed. She felt the pain leave, and by the end of the week, she brought the doctor's report. The tumors had shrunk, and one was gone!

Esther experienced the working of miracles. Shabaz experienced the gift of healing. Healing implies recovery and getting better. *"They shall lay hands on the sick, and they shall RECOVER."* (Mark 16:18)

Miracles, then, are greater in operation than the gifts of healing due to the degree of the power released in operation. I believe this has to do with the individual being ministered to. For example, we are reminded in the Scripture that Jesus himself could not perform mighty miracles in his own hometown.

> **And he could there do NO MIGHTY WORK, save that he laid his hands upon a few sick folk, and HEALED them. And he marvelled because of their unbelief. And he went round about the villages, teaching.**
>
> **Mark 6:5, 6**

I operate by this principle when there is resistance to the working of miracles in a meeting. The laying on of hands will work where there is unbelief. The sad thing is that only a few receive healing. This was true in Christ's ministry here, and we should not be surprised when it happens in our ministry to the sick and diseased.

Certainly, there was nothing wrong with Jesus' power. However, he ministered as a man with the anointing of the Holy Ghost. *"How God anointed Jesus of Nazareth with the Holy Ghost and with power: who went about doing good, and healing all that were oppressed of the devil; for God was with him"* (Acts 10:38).

Unbelief hinders miracles from taking place, but the administration of the gifts of healing by the laying on of hands worked with a "few sick folk" even when unbelief was present. The Lord began to travel and teach. Teaching the Word of God is the cure for unbelief and helps to release the gifts.

THE GIFT OF FAITH AT THE GATE CALLED BEAUTIFUL

The *gift of faith*, or special faith, is the one power gift that RECEIVES while the other two DO something. The *gift of faith,* then, is different than the other two by operation, but it is the Spirit at work in all three gifts (1 Corinthians 12:6).

I believe the Bible story in Acts 3 best illustrates the *gift of faith* as it operated in the life of Peter the day he met the crippled man when he and John went to the temple for prayer.

Peter and John were going to the temple to pray. As they were about to go into the temple, there was a crippled man who was lying at the gate called Beautiful, begging for money. He had been crippled from birth.

There was something that happened to that crippled beggar when Peter and John got him to focus on them. Now he thought it was because they were going to give him money. Peter immediately tells him we have no silver or gold for you, *but I have something!*

What Peter had was not in his hands or in his garments, but it was in him! Peter had the Spirit! He had this before the miracle took place. At that given moment, he had a special faith to release this for the crippled man.

It is wonderful to me to see how the Lord can use us if we look at adversity as an opportunity to show the world his power. Certainly, the crippled man faced a life-long crisis. He could not walk, nor was there any hope that he ever could.

There was something that Peter knew he had at that moment. It was *before* the miracle took place. We know what it was not. There was no manifestation of the utterance gifts. Peter did not give a message in tongues or interpret a message in tongues.

It was not the revelation gifts. Peter did not get a word of knowledge or wisdom. He could see that the man was crippled. The miracle had not yet taken place, nor the gift of healing released. What was it that Peter said that he had?

I believe it was the *gift of faith. The Amplified Bible* calls it *"(wonder-working) faith."* (1 Corinthians 12:9)

There by the gate called Beautiful, a crippled man received a wonderful miracle. What a contrast the Spirit gives us. The man's condition was anything but beautiful, but he sat at the entrance of the gate, which represented what God can do.

Jewish tradition tells us that each of the nine gates represented the manifestation of the nature of God. Who he is and what he can do, and what he is about to do. Isaiah the prophet typifies this gate called Beautiful with these words:

> **To appoint unto them that mourn in Zion, to give unto them BEAUTY for ashes, the oil of joy for mourning, the garment of praise for the spirit of heaviness; that they might be called trees of righteousness, the planting of the Lord, that he might be glorified.**
>
> **Isaiah 61:3**

The Lord turned the crippled man's mourning into dancing! *What you're going through does not keep you from God's BEST for your life!*

However, Peter knew he had something that would produce a miracle at that moment for the man who faced the crisis of a lifetime. Then, the Bible says that Peter took him by the hand, and immediately the crippled man's ankles were healed!

Just as the gifts of healing followed the working of miracles in (1 Corinthians 12:28) so the working of miracles followed the *gift of faith* in (Acts 3).

Certain situations place a demand on the *gift of faith*. This is true in times of danger, such as the three Hebrew boys in the fiery furnace (Daniel 3:24, 25) and in times of great need, like the prophet Elijah at the brook

Cherith (1 Kings 17:4).

Certainly, this was true that day when Peter and John ministered to the man who was crippled. What the man "expected" became the unexpected as the *gift of faith* positions us to receive God's BEST.

The *gift of faith* operated first; then came the working of miracles.

The Spirit can never be outperformed by any challenge or crisis. God is more than enough for every challenge. The *gift of faith* stands alone in operation, as do each of the other nine gifts.

Faith, or special faith, is the only one of the power gifts that *receives*, while the other two *do* something. Peter had it in operation at that moment, and it produced the miraculous! This story illustrates not only the importance of the *gift of faith* but why it is the BEST of the power gifts, especially in order of operation.

WHAT IS THE BEST GIFT?

We are instructed in the Word of God to, *"Covet earnestly THE BEST GIFTS: and yet shew I unto you a more excellent way"* (1 Corinthians 12:31).

Then notice that Paul uses the word "gifts." This seems to indicate more than one. The best gift is the one you need at that moment. We have also listed that among the three divisions or diversities of the gifts that there are certain gifts that are greater than the others in God's order of operation.

Prophecy is the greatest of the utterance gifts.

The discerning of spirits is the greatest of the revelation gifts.

Faith is the greatest of the power gifts.

Desire is born out of demonstration. I have never wanted something in life until I saw it.

When we are instructed to *"desire spiritual gifts"* (1 Corinthians 14:1), we are encouraged to *"… covet earnestly the best gifts:"* (1 Corinthians 12:31). We see then that desire is linked to seeking after the BEST gifts.

What good is a revelation without manifestation?

Then the revelation gifts and discerning of spirits, in particular, are important, but you must be able to have the manifestation of what is revealed to you, or you just have frustration. I might call someone out but do not pray for them, or even worse, there is no confirmation.

Our conclusion would be that the *gift of faith* is the greatest, and we see that it brings angels from the realms of glory to intervene on behalf of believers, as in the case of the three Hebrew boys (Daniel 3:25), Daniel in the lion's den (Daniel 6:22), and Paul in the great storm. (Acts 27:23)

One of the characteristics of the *gift of faith* is that supernatural peace will come to you in the midst of a crisis. Peter, in prison, slept in peace the night before his execution. (Acts 12:6)

Acts 3 shows us that the *gift of faith* is the greatest of the gifts in the general sense, remembering that the greatest gift is the one needed at the moment. The importance of knowing this has to do with praying and desiring the best gift in our lives.

> **Delight thyself also in the Lord; and he shall give thee the DESIRES of thine heart.**
> **Psalm 37:4**

> **Therefore I say unto you, What things soever ye DESIRE, when ye pray, believe that ye receive them, and ye shall have them.**
> **Mark 11:24**

The *gift of faith,* then, is for supernatural power (Acts 3, Acts 19:11, 12)

The *gift of faith* is for supernatural provision. (Exodus 16:15, 1 Kings 17:4, Psalm 3:5)

The *gift of faith* is for supernatural protection. (Daniel 3:25, Daniel 6:22, Acts 12:6, Acts 27)

The *gift of faith* is for supernatural promotion. (Genesis 27:28, 29, Genesis 50:24, 25)

My father had a saying he taught me and my brothers, *"Good, better, best. Never let it rest until your good is better and your better is BEST!"*

CHAPTER 2

What is the Gift of Faith?

> To another faith by the same Spirit; 1 Corinthians 12:9

The Church's greatest need is the gift of faith. The spirit of anti-Christ is manifesting all around the world. Doubts and fears are everywhere, unbelief and dismay as well. The devil knows his time is short. *"Therefore rejoice, O heavens, and you who dwell in them! Woe to the inhabitants of the earth and the sea! For the devil has come down to you, having great wrath, because he knows that he has a short time"* (Revelation 12:12).

Our prayer is – open the windows of Heaven – increase our faith – give us God's faith. Then we will be able to operate in this gift of faith which raises the dead, gives personal protection, brings supernatural provision, and helps to cast out devils.

Definition: The gift of faith is the ability given by the Spirit to the believer to receive the faith of God in the present moment for supernatural provision and protection. It is God in you, believing through you and for you.

Weymouth, in his commentary, calls it "special faith." The Amplified Bible refers to it as [wonder-working faith].

The gift of faith is the first of the three power gifts listed in (1 Corinthians 12). This gift may be the greatest of the three. The gift of faith may be needed now more than ever. The Bible seems to indicate that it came upon God's servants in times of danger, crisis, and trouble.

Lester Sumrall said, "This gift of faith operates through the power of the Holy Spirit for the performance of supernatural exploits."

The gift of faith makes you more than a conqueror on every occasion.

> **Nay, in all these things we are more than CONQUERORS through him that loved us.**
> **Romans 8:37**

All things are possible to a man or woman of faith. This gift of "special faith" can move mountains, turn darkness into day, and send devils and diseases back to hell.

Howard Carter wrote this about the gift of faith:

> This gift can "minister the Spirit" imparting the holy fullness which is the "promise of the Father," enriching the soul and empowering it for spiritual service. By this gift, blessings can be pronounced which miraculously and permanently change the whole course of one's career.[1]

I believe this is what happened to me.

EVANGELIST R. W. SCHAMBACH

"You don't have any trouble. All you need is faith in God!" This was my last lesson of the day in my dorm room at Bible school. The classroom was coming over my portable radio. My teacher was R. W. Schambach. I would tune in to the 50,000-watt superpower radio station WWVA every night for those three years.

Then the day came that I could attend a Schambach Miracle Revival service in Boston, Massachusetts, in

---

1. Carter, Howard. *Questions and Answers on the Gifts of the Spirit.* Harrison House, 1991.

the John Hancock Hall. The song leader led us in powerful, upbeat singing. The organ blared and tambourines shook. It was wonderful. Then, I saw a man in a long winter coat walk down the far aisle carrying a briefcase. You could feel something about him.

He went to the platform and took his coat off. He picked up a tambourine and joined in the worship. The only way I can describe it is the atmosphere shifted, and it was filled with the anointing when suddenly a man screamed out and ran to the front of the auditorium. I smelled the alcohol on him as he passed by my seat.

Brother Schambach jumped down and laid his hands on the man. "Come out, you demon of lust for alcohol!" There was a brief scream, and the man was free. My friend from Zion Gospel Temple had stood up behind the man to assist Brother Schambach. He told me later there was a strong smell of alcohol that filled the air, and then it was gone! The man was clean and sober, and Brother Schambach led him to the Lord right there.

He took the microphone and began to preach. He preached on "A Double Portion." Then a prayer line was formed, and he began to lay his hands on the people. When I came through, he stopped the prayer line, and with those piercing eyes, he looked at me and said,

"What do you want?" I told him, "Twice as much as what you have!" He then laid his hands upon me that night almost forty-nine years ago, and when he did, something from him came into me by the power of the Holy Ghost!

Then as I went to go to my seat, Brother Schambach grabbed me and said, "Stand by my side and help me pray for the people." After the service that night, he asked me who I was. When I told him, he said, "You're that little boy?!" My father had pastored his family in Harrisburg First Assembly. The last time that I saw him was at his sister's home going. We had stood together at the graveside. We were the last two to leave. He was an older seasoned evangelist, and I was a teenager.

Now we were joined together again. God was working out his plan, and because I put a demand on his anointing, I had the privilege of standing with him for over thirty-eight years of friendship and fellowship.

R.W. Schambach taught me everything that I learned about the deliverance ministry and miracle evangelism. The gift of faith he operated in was contagious. I saw the gift of faith in a man.

THE GIFT OF FAITH IS FOR YOU

Nothing is impossible when you put your trust in God! God has what you need when you need it. This is never truer than in times of trouble. The Scriptures remind us:

> **God is our refuge and strength, A VERY PRESENT HELP IN TROUBLE.**
> **Psalm 46:1**

There are nine gifts of the Spirit, which are listed in 1 Corinthians 12. The gift of faith is the only gift listed that is *for* you, and all of the other gifts work *through* you to bless or help others.

When we are confronted with what seems to be impossible situations, the gift of faith makes the impossible possible! One of the greatest definitions of how the power gifts work is found in the book of Acts.

> **And BY THE HANDS OF THE APOSTLES were many SIGNS and WONDERS wrought among the people. And they were all with one accord in Solomon's porch.**
> **Acts 5:12**

It is God's supernatural power working through natural men and women. It is the wonderful Holy Spirit giving you and me the ability to be in service for the Lord Jesus Christ. We must remember that the power comes from him and walk humbly before him.

> **But we have this treasure in earthen vessels, that the excellency of the power may be of God, and not of us.**
> **2 Corinthians 4:7**

We are the vessels he chooses to use, but it is God's power that accomplishes his will. The Holy Spirit gets the job done through human vessels and by their hands. Your hands are a part of your body, so we can say the Lord uses the body of Christ to show his power. It is Christ in us who does the work.

I RECEIVED THE GIFT OF FAITH IN A BLIZZARD

People have asked me, "What was the greatest miracle that you have ever seen?" My wife and I have seen the Lord do many mighty things. He has opened the eyes of the blind, caused deaf ears to hear, the crippled have walked, and cancers have disappeared. He has done so many great things! The greatest by far was the night he raised up my son.

A blizzard was roaring through Indiana, and it hit while my wife and I were holding a revival at Clay City Assembly of God. The church was founded by Reverend Lexie Allen, the wife of evangelist A. A. Allen.

Our son was not yet one year old when a terrible fever and congestion attacked his little body. We were staying in a room off of the church gymnasium. The heat was poor, and he began to choke and turn blue. My wife awakened me, and I saw the situation was critical. He was not breathing properly. The hospital in Indianapolis was over an hour away, but the roads were closed due to the storm.

I picked him up in my arms and wrapped him in his little blue blanket. My wife walked with me out into the gym, trying to clear his nose so that he could breathe. I felt fear and helplessness take hold of my mind. My prayer was very short, "Oh Lord, please help my boy."

Suddenly, I knew that God would touch him and that he would be alright. He sneezed like the little boy in the Bible.

> **Then the child sneezed seven times, and the child opened his eyes.**
> **2 Kings 4:35**

I looked down, and his nose began to run, and the fever went out of his body. He fell asleep in my arms, and his face was red. My wife put him back in his little bed, and we fell asleep. The next morning he woke us up, holding to the crib and jumping. The sun was shining, and the storm was over in more ways than one!

The Lord gave my wife a word that we use constantly to remind us of God's Help. "There is nothing that can happen to me that God can't do something about it!"

> **Where there is no vision, the people perish:**
> **Proverbs 29:18**

You must take your eyes off of your problem. The trouble that tells you that nothing is going to change and that you are going to remain in that condition for the rest of your life, plagued by despair and hopelessness.

C.M. Ward, a preacher and friend of my father, used to say, "We have too many cross-eyed Christians. One eye is on the Cross and the other on their troubles." When the gift of faith is in operation, then you realize,

You don't have a CRISIS; you have a CHRIST!

The Bible shows us what to do:

> **LOOKING UNTO JESUS, the author and finisher of our faith, who for the joy that was set before him endured the Cross, despising the shame, and has sat down at the right hand of the throne of God.**
>
> **Hebrews 12:2**

Jesus had just raised Lazarus from the dead. The Lord now had come up to Jerusalem for the Passover Feast. He sent his disciples to get a young donkey and rode into the city. The people went out to meet him and started shouting, *"Blessed is he who comes in the name of the Lord! The King of Israel!"* (John 12:13)

Certain disciples began telling how the Lord had raised Lazarus from the dead. It was for this reason, the crowd went out to see him. The Pharisees saw it as being futile, but the Greeks ran out to see him, who had done this thing. Their desire should be ours as well, *"WE WISH TO SEE JESUS."*

THE GIFT OF FAITH IN THE BIG APPLE

New York City is sometimes called the Big Apple. Years after I had attended the meeting in Boston, I found myself working with the man of God. He and I were eating at a diner, and I asked him about where I should start on the radio. Brother Schambach told me that if you can get a breakthrough in New York City, then you can be used anywhere for God's glory. He loved New York.

One night, he called me into the trailer behind the tent. He told me, "Tonight, God is going to heal people out of wheelchairs!" He instructed me to go out under the tent and find everyone that was in a wheelchair and place them up front to the left of the platform. Then he said, "I will come down the ramp, and we will pray for them because God is going to heal them tonight!"

The song leader started the praise and worship. Several thousand happy people began to sing and give God the Glory. Brother Schambach came out onto the platform. My mind went back to the meeting in Boston. It was the same atmosphere. He started to pace the platform like a lion. He caught my eyes and then took the microphone.

"God's gonna empty them wheelchairs tonight! Get ready, beloved." He said, "You ready, Brother Shuttlesworth?" He was always respectful. He could have called me Ted. I would have answered him. Here he came down the ramp. I saw a change come on his countenance. He stood in front of the people in the wheelchairs and said, "Look at me! You are coming out of those wheelchairs tonight!"

I thought of Peter and John. *"Look on us!"*

There was an elderly Chinese woman in the first wheelchair. She was the first one that I brought down. She could not speak English, but her daughter could. The daughter had told me earlier that her mother had not walked for twenty years. Brother Schambach took her by the hand and shouted, "Walk, Momma!" Suddenly she shook under the power and rose up! She took off walking, and the daughter was pushing the empty wheelchair trying to catch up with her mother.

The next was a West Indian man. He had told me that he had neuropathy from diabetes. Our evangelist laid hands on him then he told me, "Get him out of that wheelchair!" The man had already told me that it had been several years since he walked, I took ahold of him, and he stood, unsteady at first, then he lifted his hands and praised the Lord.

The Lord emptied six wheelchairs that night. The gift of faith came on the evangelist in the trailer, then the power of the Holy Ghost came on the crippled, just like in Bible days.

I saw the gift of faith in a man for God's glory!

THE DIFFERENCE BETWEEN THE GIFT OF FAITH AND THE WORKING OF MIRACLES

The gift of faith RECEIVES something, whereas the working of miracles DOES something. They are different in operation but with the same results. This is best illustrated in the Bible stories of Daniel (Daniel 6:22) and Samson (Judges 14:6). They both dealt with dangerous lions.

The gift of faith is passive and helps us to receive the working of miracles.

God performed a miracle for Daniel in a time of great danger. Daniel did nothing but BELIEVE his God, and he was delivered.

> **Then was the king exceeding glad for him, and commanded that they should take Daniel up out of the den. So Daniel was taken up out of the den, and no manner of hurt was found upon him, because he BELIEVED in his God.**
> **Daniel 6:23**

The working of miracles is active.

Samson was confronted by a lion in the vineyards of Timnath. He killed it with his bare hands when the Spirit of the Lord came upon him.

> **And the Spirit of the Lord came mightily upon him, and he rent him as he would have rent a kid (a young goat), and he had nothing in his hand: but he told not his father or his mother what he had done.**
>
> **Judges 14:6**

God formed the world out of nothing by his mighty hand. *"Through FAITH, we understand that the worlds were framed by the Word of God, so that things which are seen were not made of things which do appear."* (Hebrews 11:3) It is this divine order and plan of God for creation that the devil attacks.

All FAITH comes from God. The verse that best explains faith to me is *"With men, this is impossible, but with God, ALL things are possible"* (Matthew 19:26).

Again the Bible seems to indicate that it came upon God's servants in times of crisis and trouble.

There are different aspects to this God-like faith. Only two times is the word faith found in the Old Testament. *"The just shall live by his FAITH"* (Habakkuk 2:4). and God's reprimand to Israel. *"Children in whom is no FAITH"* (Deuteronomy 32:20). This shows us that the Lord expects us to live and operate by our faith.

The New Testament has 280 references to faith. The Pauline revelation gives us an understanding of the different kinds of faith and the guidelines for their operation. When I was younger, I played baseball, football, and basketball. They are all "ball" games, but each has different rules that govern them, and so it is with faith.

CHAPTER 3
The 4 Kinds of Bible Faith

The *gift of faith*, as in all the gifts of the Spirit, is supernatural. It is important to understand that there are different kinds of faith that are mentioned in the Bible as well as different degrees of the operation of faith that we walk in. Since it was God's eternal purpose that the just live by faith (Habakkuk 2:4), we see the greatest release of this was after the work of the Cross. It takes what Jesus did on the Cross to produce the God-kind of faith. It begins at salvation.

1. Faith for salvation

The only faith that a sinner can have is faith for salvation. *"Now we know that God heareth not sinners:"* (John 9:31). The Psalmist knew, *"If I regard iniquity in my heart, the Lord will not hear me:"* (Psalm 66:18). The only prayer that the Lord responds to in the case of the sinner is the prayer of repentance.

We read in Acts 16 of the salvation of the Philippian jailer. His question was, *"Sirs, what must I do to be saved?"* Paul and Silas answered, *"Believe on the Lord Jesus Christ, and thou shalt be saved, and thy house"* (Acts 16:30, 31).

The two elements of faith for salvation are confession and believing.

> **That if thou shalt CONFESS with thy mouth the Lord Jesus, and shalt BELIEVE in thine heart that God hath raised him from the dead, thou shalt be saved.**
> **Romans 10:9**

> **For by grace are ye saved through FAITH, and that not of yourselves: it is the gift of God.**
> **Ephesians 2:8**

THE RICKSHAW CYCLIST IN INDIA

The Lord taught me a valuable lesson in India in 1981. A rickshaw cyclist picked me up to take me to my hotel. When I got in the back of the carriage, I asked him, "Do you know Jesus?" His answer was, "No. Tell me where he lives, and I will take you there."

If he could have done that, we both would have been surprised! He heard the Gospel for the first time that day. There are so many who have never heard the story of Christ.

The great Canadian pastor, Oswald J. Smith, said, "Why should anyone hear the Gospel twice before everyone has heard it once?"

> **The fruit of the righteous is a tree of life; and he that winneth souls is wise.**
> **Proverbs 11:30**

Jesus commanded us to *"Go ye into all the world, and preach the Gospel to every creature."* (Mark 16:15). Salvation is a gift from God. It comes by hearing the Word of God. You have got to tell it for saving faith to work.

In a message at the London Metropolitan Tabernacle, Charles Spurgeon said, "We are not responsible to God for the souls that are saved, but we are responsible for the Gospel that is preached, and for the way in which we preach it."

The Bible indicates that a person is used to preach the Word to bring about this kind of saving faith (1 Corinthians 1:21; Romans 10:14), whereas the gift of faith is given by the Spirit directly to the believer without the aid of man.

2. Faith for our daily walk

> **But without faith it is impossible to please him: for he that cometh to God must believe that he is, and that he is a rewarder of them that diligently seek him.**
> **Hebrews 11:6**

I chose this as my life's Scripture when I was in Bible school. It reminds us that we are to please the Lord in our daily lives. God requires us to live by faith. This kind of faith is a choice. You choose to serve the Lord. We walk it out on a daily basis.

We live daily for the Lord by dying daily to the flesh. Paul reminds us, *"I die daily."* (1 Corinthians 15:31). We are reminded that *"So then they that are in the flesh cannot please God"* (Romans 8:8).

The walk of faith has nothing to do with the natural fleshly senses. Remember, *"for we walk by faith, not by sight"* (2 Corinthians 5:7). It is this kind of faith that obtains the promises of God's Word.

God tells us in his Word that we cannot please him without faith (Hebrews 11:6). It would be unfair of the

Lord to require us to have this kind of faith if he also did not give us the means to receive it.

The eleventh chapter of Hebrews begins with the reminder that, *"For by it the elders obtained a good report,"* and concludes with, *"And these all, having obtained a good report through faith, received not the promise: God having provided some better thing for us, that they without us should not be made perfect"* (Hebrews 11:2, 39, 40).

We can say then that all faith is a gift of God.

> **God hath dealt to every man the measure of FAITH.**
> **Romans 12:3**

There is only one way that faith is given to us; *"So then faith cometh by hearing, and hearing by the word of God"* (Romans 10:17). The believer has a measure of faith given to them by the Lord through the hearing of his Word and that faith can grow and be increased.

> **We are bound to thank God always for you, brethren, as it is meet, because that your FAITH GROWETH exceedingly, and the charity of every one of you all toward each other aboundeth;**
> **2 Thessalonians 1:3**

We receive answers to prayer by this kind of faith. *"And the PRAYER OF FAITH shall save the sick, and the Lord shall raise him up; and if he has committed sins, they shall be forgiven him."* (James 5:15)

I once read that one minister called this "general faith" and that this is how we receive answers to prayer. Again Jesus encourages us, *"Therefore I say unto you, what things soever ye desire, when ye pray, believe that ye receive them, and ye shall have them."* (Mark 11:24)

The *gift of faith* is given to us by the Spirit immediately, but the walk of faith is a lifetime of dedication as we determine to do the will of God. It is a spiritual exercise and is not determined by our natural senses. *"...For we walk by faith and not by sight."* (2 Corinthians 5:7)

3. Faith as a fruit of the Spirit

The Old Testament refers to "faith" only two times, but the word "faithful" and "faithfulness" is found a total of 73 times. All of the gifts of the Spirit are for service to mankind. *"But by love serve one another."* (Galatians 5:13). It is love which is the first of the fruit of the Spirit.

The fruit of the Spirit is then for the individual who would serve mankind. Jesus taught, *"Wherefore by their fruits ye shall know them."* (Matthew 7:20). The fruit of the Spirit are the counterbalance to the gifts of the Spirit. We are reminded:

> **But the fruit of the Spirit is love, joy, peace, longsuffering, gentleness, goodness, FAITH . . .**
> **Galatians 5:22**

Fruit can grow. When we say "I believe God," the strength of that confession should grow stronger the longer we serve the Lord. Faithfulness, or the fruit of faith, comes from a lifetime of serving the Lord. This is defined by the Scripture:

> **His lord said unto him, Well done, good and faithful servant; thou hast been FAITHFUL over a few things, I will make thee RULER over many things: enter thou into the joy of thy lord.**
> **Matthew 25:23**

The fruit of faith brings honor to a believer. When we study the Scripture concerning this matter, we find that Paul taught Timothy, *"If a man therefore purge himself from these, he shall be a vessel unto HONOUR, sanctified, and meet for the master's use, and prepared unto every good work."* (2 Timothy 2:21)

> The gift of faith is for power,
> and the fruit of faith is for character.

THE CALCUTTA STORY

Calcutta! This is the city named for the Hindu goddess of death, Kali. It sits on the banks of the Hooghly River. When I was there, nine million people were jammed into an area of less than thirty-seven square miles. Today it has a population of almost fifteen million.

One minister that had visited there called it an "outpost of hell." Jesus loves Calcutta, and when I was invited to travel there and preach, I went. The Lord allowed me to meet the Canadian couple, Mark and Huldah Buntain. God's Light-Bearers!

Their day began in prayer at 4:30 am. Then they went to their food distribution at one of the many feeding stations where over 12,000 people, mainly children, were fed at least one meal a day. We went to the school that trained young men and women's minds with Christian education. A print shop, trade school, and hospital filled their days with the work of the Lord.

When I preached at the church on Royd Street, I knew

that I did not have the depth of character or commitment that these folks had, but I wanted what they had. I met Mother Theresa, whose work was down the street. The Buntains and this little woman had something in common — a beautiful, sweet, and kind spirit as they ministered to the poor and needy.

I witnessed the fruit of faith in these precious folks that came from a lifetime of faithful service. Paul wrote:

> **And I thank Christ Jesus our Lord, who hath enabled me, for that he counted me FAITHFUL, putting me into the ministry;**
> **1 Timothy 1:12**

4. Faith as the gift of the Spirit

> **To another faith by the same Spirit;**
> **1 Corinthians 12:9**

When we examine this gift, we see the following characteristics revealed: it works as the Spirit wills, and it is profitable. The Lord disperses it by the Holy Spirit to a believer. It falls within the division of the power gifts.

We understand then that the gift of faith *receives* from the Lord.

The gift of faith overcomes demonic plans of confusion by bringing your life into alignment with the will of God. *"For God is not the author of confusion, but of peace, as it is in all churches of the saints"* (1 Corinthians 14:33).

The gift of faith brings you supernatural peace in the midst of a crisis.

The gift of faith brings order out of chaos. There is a divine order concerning the operation of the gifts of the Spirit. *"Let all things be done decently and in order"* (1 Corinthians 14:40).

God desires to enable his children to rise to any occasion that confronts them with the thought of overcoming that situation. God has what you need when you need it. This is never more true than in times of trouble. The Scriptures remind us, *"God is our refuge and strength, A VERY PRESENT HELP IN TROUBLE"* (Psalm 46:1).

We are the vessels he chooses to use, but it is God's power that accomplishes his will. The Holy Spirit gets the job done through human vessels and by their hands. Your hands are a part of your body, so we can say the Lord uses the body of Christ to show his power. It is Christ in us who does the work.

THE GIFT OF FAITH KEPT ME ON TELEVISION

I was holding a meeting in Sarnia, Ontario. My son and I were working together there in a convention. The Lord was moving and confirming his Word with signs following (Mark 16:20). The Lord opened the eyes of a totally blind woman on the opening Sunday morning.

I held two services a day, and I taught on the gift of faith in the day services. I was on my way to the auditorium on Tuesday morning when I received a call from Eric Smith, our media buyer. He told me, "Brother Ted, I hate to tell you this, but you have been canceled on your largest network. It has been sold."

The largest network that we were on had canceled our program without the standard four-week notification. There were tens of thousands who were calling us in a year's time. Suddenly, it was over . . . or was it?

A supernatural peace came upon me, and a special faith rose up inside of my spirit.

I told him we would buy time on two other networks, which we did, and we have never missed a week of preaching the Gospel on television for the last twenty-one years. We cover the world by television in over 200 nations every week. Praise God for his faithfulness.

The gift of faith brings a good conclusion in times of crisis. You will be challenged by the devil if you would live for God, but no matter what the devil brings your way to discourage or destroy you, this gift ensures victory always!

CHAPTER 4
Courage in the Time of Crisis

There is a holy indignation that comes up in my spirit when I hear people say, "The struggle is real," because those words discount the Lord's power to turn trouble into triumph.

When you emphasize the problems of life as being insurmountable, you discredit the overcoming power of the Spirit. The gift of faith is the Spirit's power given to every believer, no matter what the difficulty, that guarantees victory in life.

> **For whatsoever is born of God OVERCOMETH the world: and this is the victory that OVERCOMETH the world, even our faith.**
>
> 1 John 5:4

The gifts of the Spirit help us to supernaturally overcome the devil's actions which are designed to destroy the believer.

The gift of faith is designed to bring victory in times of crisis and danger. I remember reading a book by a minister some years ago where he stated, "The gift of faith is given in times of danger or distress."

One of the characteristics of the gift of faith is that a supernatural peace will come on you in the midst of crisis. It produces peace and calm in the midst of turmoil and challenge. It can be activated when danger is present. I call it courage in the time of crisis!

The gift of faith is a part of God's unlimited ability or power given to the believer at the moment of need to achieve what the Lord wants to be done through the life of that person. It is not a feeling. It is more of a knowing.

The gift of faith, more than any other of the nine gifts of the Spirit, has angels associated with the release of this gift. It is the Spirit that causes all the gifts to operate. However, angels were present many times in the administration and release of the gift of faith to God's servants. We see angels on assignment in the stories of Gideon, Daniel, the three Hebrew children, Peter, and Paul.

> **Are they not all ministering spirits, sent forth to minister FOR THEM who shall be heirs of salvation?**
>
> **Hebrews 1:14**

AN ANGEL AT THE MARINE BASE

Time has brought to me many things that are hard to explain. I believe that I saw an angel in my hotel room near Camp Lejeune in North Carolina in the 1970s. The story actually began in Pennsylvania a few months before.

While we were fasting and praying for the meeting, the Lord came to me in prayer, and a story began to unfold in my mind. These were the thoughts that he gave me. "A pastor and his wife are coming to the parsonage with a baby. Go downstairs and tell them I will heal the child."

Just then, the doorbell rang, and I heard the voices of people talking to the pastor. I arose and went downstairs, and there stood this couple, and the mother was holding a newborn baby in her arms. When I told her I would pray for her baby, she screamed, "Don't touch my baby!"

The child had been diagnosed with a rare skin disorder where the flesh would come off, and there would be bleeding. It was a life-threatening disease. I was not allowed to pray for the child even though I tried to assure them that the Lord had spoken to me to do so. They were both wonderful ministers. The Lord wanted to heal their baby. I had not seen them in years, nor did I know that she had just had this child. I felt like I failed God.

Now, a few months later, I was in Jacksonville, North Carolina, holding a meeting, and my wife and I were staying at a Host Inn off of Route 17. The night before the meetings started, I woke up and saw a tall man looking at me. He stood erect, and I felt no danger. For a moment, I thought a Marine had come into the room. Then he disappeared!

My heart was racing, so I got out of bed and knelt to pray for the meetings. My thoughts were drawn back to the failure I had experienced in Pennsylvania, and my prayer was, "Lord, use me in a greater way."

Then, the very next day, a woman came and brought me her child with the exact same skin disorder that the baby had in Pennsylvania! Her boy had special coverings on his little arms and body. Suddenly, I felt a strong sense of boldness or courage come upon me. Gently, I prayed for the little boy.

The mother returned that night and told us that new skin seemed to have come on his little body. She had removed the coverings, and the discoloration was gone. He continued to improve that week.

As I look back and weave those two exact conditions of the two boys together in my mind, I have come to the conclusion that the angelic visitation gave me an operation of the gift of faith for that skin disorder. My thoughts after the angel left had turned to Pennsylvania, not knowing that the very next day, I would encounter the same thing again.

The importance of the gift of faith is that it aids in supernatural protection and provision, and there seems to be the accompanying ministry of angels with this gift.

THE NIGHT AN ANGEL APPEARED TO GIDEON

An angel appears to Gideon. The angel spoke these words, *"The Lord is with thee, thou mighty man of valour."* (Judges 6:12). One commentary says that the angel pronounced Gideon a warrior and hero. Then Gideon is prompted to ask this question, *"And where be all his MIRACLES which our fathers told us of,"* (Judges 6:13)

Gideon's response was we need miracles to deliver us out of the hands of the Midianites. When Gideon received the word of the angel that night, it produced the gift of faith. The miracle had not happened yet, but it would come to pass. He was given the ability to deal with the crisis of the Midianites' invasion.

Israel's danger activated the ministry of angels at that moment which caused a transformation of the human condition as the Holy Spirit released the gift of faith. It took Gideon from fearfully hiding by a winepress threshing wheat to the front lines of battle thrashing the enemy.

> **Then Gideon built an altar there unto the Lord, and called it Jehovah-shalom: unto this day it is yet in Ophrah of the Abi-ezrites.**
>
> **Judges 6:24**

God had now revealed himself as the God of peace. Gideon, who felt like the least member of a poor family, was suddenly transformed into a man of valor, a hero, a mighty warrior. He now found peace in the time of danger, whereas before, he fearfully threshed wheat in the darkness of night. Supernatural peace is now released by the gift of faith.

> **But the Spirit of the Lord came upon Gideon.**
>
> **Judges 6:34**

Gideon then intensified in strength and power that proved greater than the entire host of Midian and the Amalekites. God destroyed the oppressor, and the danger was over. Peace then ruled the land. He received courage in the time of crisis!

AN ANGEL IN THE DEN OF LIONS

One day, there is coming a great meeting in the air! I look forward to seeing Daniel someday. Here is a man who stayed true to God in the most adverse circumstances. He literally put his life on the line for Jehovah and was in imminent danger for doing so.

Daniel's early life began with the Babylonians' invasion of Jerusalem, and then he was taken into captivity in Babylon. He was given favor in the eyes of his master. Because of that favor, he was promoted to ruler over the whole province of Babylon (Daniel 2:38).

We see that Daniel had *"an excellent spirit"* in him. (Daniel 6:3). He served three kings but worshipped only one God. Nebuchadnezzar, Belshazzar, and Darius all saw what Daniel knew *"But there is a God in heaven that revealeth secrets"* (Daniel 2:28).

The more that God uses you, the more you will deal with the jealousy of men. The Apostle Paul dealt with this, and he reminded us that he was *"in perils among false brethren;* (2 Corinthians 11:26).

Daniel's ability to interpret the dreams of Nebuchadnezzar (Daniel 2:27-45; 4:19-32), the handwriting on the wall for Belshazzar (Daniel 5:23-30), the understanding of the word of the Lord that came to Jeremiah in the first year of Darius, the king (Daniel 9:2) and his visions in the third year of Cyrus (Daniel 10) brought threat and danger to him.

> **Then the presidents and princes sought to FIND OCCASION against Daniel concerning the kingdom; but they could find none occasion nor fault; forasmuch as he was faithful, neither was there any error or fault found in him.**
>
> **Daniel 6:4**

The believer who seeks to be used by God will be opposed by false brethren and demon powers. Daniel's faithfulness to walk before the Lord and pray brought him from his lofty position as the top president of three (Daniel 6:2) to a den of lions (Daniel 6:16).

The devil hates those who are faithful to the Lord and seek to demonstrate his power. We are engaged in warfare (Ephesians 6:12). However, it is the one fight we cannot lose, and the one fight the devil can never win.

FIGHT THE GOOD FIGHT OF FAITH, lay hold on eternal life, whereunto thou art also called, and hast professed a good profession before many witnesses.
                                1 Timothy 6:12

We are reminded that we are to *"Be sober, be vigilant; because your adversary the devil, as a ROARING LION, walketh about, seeking whom he may devour:"* (1 Peter 5:8).

R. W. Schambach used to say, "When the devil starts messing, the Lord starts blessing! Your elder brother Jesus rendered the devil helpless on the Cross over two thousand years ago. Jesus pulled his teeth out at the Cross. The only thing that the devil can do now is roar and gum you to death."

Later, we discover that behind the scenes of the supernatural, Daniel's real threat was a demonic power, *"the prince of the kingdom of Persia"* (Daniel 10:13). Could it be that this is why angels operate with the gift of faith? I believe this gift brings angels to help us.

Daniel had to deal with the Prince of Persia, an evil spirit that ruled over Persia. The angel that came to Daniel also refers to the archangel Michael coming to help (Daniel 10:13). We see it took two angels from Heaven to drive back the demonic Prince of Persia, who was a ruler over this region.

Perhaps this was the angel that supernaturally protected Daniel in the den of lions. The day came when Daniel was cast into the den of lions. The king testified, *"Thy God whom thou servest continually, he will deliver thee"* (Daniel 6:16).

A stone was placed over the mouth of the den. The foul, hot breath of these man-killers filled the atmosphere, and Daniel was fully committed to God's delivering power. The morning dawn bathed the landscape, and the king hurried to the den. His broken-hearted cry was, is your God able to deliver you from the lions?

> **MY GOD HATH SENT HIS ANGEL, and hath shut the lions' mouths, that they have not hurt me: forasmuch as before him innocency was found in me; and also before thee, O king, have I done no hurt.**
>
> **Daniel 6:22**

How did this miracle take place? We read that:

> **Then was the king exceeding glad for him, and commanded that they should take Daniel up out of the den. So Daniel was taken up out of the den, and no**

> manner of hurt was found upon him, because HE BELIEVED in his God.
> Daniel 6:23

The gift of faith is an unwavering belief that is activated in times of crisis and danger.

THE THREE HEBREW CHILDREN

When you read the book of Daniel, it is evident that there is great spiritual opposition from the enemy when he comes to hinder your dedication and walk with God. That is never more so than in the story of the three Hebrew children.

Nebuchadnezzar had been troubled by a dream (Daniel 2:3). Daniel came and interpreted the dream and described the image of a man with a head of gold. Daniel told him that he was that golden head (Daniel 2:37, 38).

The gods of Babylon, the soothsayers, and magicians were powerless to help interpret Nebuchadnezzar's dream, but Daniel knew, *"there is a God in heaven that revealeth secrets."*

> Then Daniel went to his house, and made the thing known to HANANIAH,

> **MISHAEL, and AZARIAH, his companions: That they would desire mercies of the God of heaven concerning this secret; that Daniel and his fellows should not perish with the rest of the wise men of Babylon.**
>
> **Daniel 2:17, 18**

Why did the Babylonians change the names of the Hebrew children, and why did Daniel refer to them by their Hebrew names when it was time to seek the Lord? Was it because their Hebrew names referred to the one true living God and their Babylonian referred to the names of false gods who are not gods?

Was it because there is no help from false gods and idols but *"Our soul waiteth for the Lord: he is our help and our shield." (Psalm 33:20)*?

I believe it was because their names glorified the one true living God.

DANIEL'S name meant "God is my Judge." They changed Daniel's name to "Belteshazzar," which meant "Bel (their god) will protect."

HANANIAH'S name meant "God has been gracious." They renamed him Shadrach, which meant "inspired of Aku."

MISHAEL in Hebrew meant, "Who is what God is." Meshach represented the false god Aku with the thought "Mishael belonged to Aku."

AZARIAH was "God has helped." Abed-nego meant "servant, or slave, of Nego."

When they received an answer from God during this time when their lives were threatened, it was at that moment the gift of faith was in operation.

THE ANGEL IN THE FIERY FURNACE

Nebuchadnezzar then built an idol of gold based on Daniel's interpretation. Paul tells us that idolatry has a spirit that leads men away from God (1 Corinthians 12:2). One of the works of the last days is seducing spirits that create doctrines of devils to deceive the people (1 Timothy 4:1).

Satan's age-old sin is he desires worship. Isaiah 14 reveals this satanic pride, and in fact, Isaiah refers to this spirit as the *"king of Babylon:"* (Isaiah 14:4). I have no question that it was Lucifer himself behind the motive for Nebuchadnezzar to create this idol. The devil always perverts the Word of God. He wants all worship directed to him and away from the one, true living God.

The devil even tempted Christ to worship him.

> **If thou therefore wilt WORSHIP ME, all shall be thine. And Jesus answered and said unto him, Get thee behind me, Satan: for it is written, THOU SHALT WORSHIP THE LORD THY GOD, AND HIM ONLY shalt thou serve.**
> **Luke 4:7, 8**

Nebuchadnezzar set up the golden image. Musicians gathered to play for this ungodly hour when the people were to bow down and worship. Three Hebrew boys refused to bow down before the idol. Informers turned them in. The king called for them to come.

His challenge was filled with the contempt of pride and the arrogance of power *"Who is that God that shall deliver you out of my hands?"* (Daniel 3:15).

They had received the gift of faith before when they agreed that Daniel would receive the interpretation of Nebuchadnezzar's dream.

They knew that their God would deliver them. They were not talking about Bel, Aku, or Nego, the false gods of Babylon. Their testimony was,

> **If it be so, OUR GOD WHOM WE SERVE IS ABLE TO DELIVER us from the burning fiery furnace, and he will deliver us out of thine hand, O king.**
>
> **Daniel 3:17**

They received their deliverance *before* they were cast into the fiery furnace. This is the gift of faith in operation. They believed their God was able. Let Nebuchadnezzar heat the furnace seven times hotter; our God is able to deliver us.

My Dad used to preach, "If you bow, you will burn; but if you do not bow, then you will not burn."

They cast them into the fiery furnace. The king came to see what had happened. The Bible records these faith-building words:

> **He answered and said, Lo, I see four men loose, walking in the midst of the fire, and they have no hurt; and the form of THE FOURTH IS LIKE THE SON OF GOD.**
>
> **Daniel 3:25**

I had the honor of being with Oral Roberts in Dallas, Texas, in 1990. He shared several things with me about ministry. He spoke of having "fire in your belly" when you preach. He would not leave his room to go and preach until it stirred up in him.

His message "The Fourth Man" was not only one of his greatest faith messages, but it caused the gift of faith to operate in him for the working of miracles. Here in part, is that message in which he emphasized Christ in every book of the Bible.

WHO IS THIS FOURTH MAN?

In Genesis, he is the Seed of the Woman.

In Exodus, he is the Passover Lamb.

In Leviticus, he is our High Priest.

In Numbers, he is the Pillar of Cloud by day and the Pillar of Fire by night.

In Deuteronomy, he is the Prophet like unto Moses.

In Joshua, he is the Captain of our Salvation.

In Judges, he is our Judge and Lawgiver.

In Ruth, he is our Kinsman Redeemer.

In 1 and 2 Samuel, he is our Trusted Prophet.

In Kings and Chronicles, he is our Reigning King. In Ezra, he is the Rebuilder of the Broken Down Walls of Human Life.

In Esther, he is our Mordecai.

In Job, he is our Ever-Living Redeemer, "for I know

my Redeemer liveth."

Who is this fourth man?

In Psalms, he is our Shepherd.

In Proverbs and Ecclesiastes, he is our Wisdom.

In the Song of Solomon, he is our Lover and Bridegroom.

In Isaiah, he is the Prince of Peace.

In Jeremiah, he is the Righteous Branch.

In Lamentations, he is our Weeping Prophet.

In Ezekiel, he is the wonderful Four-Faced Man.

In Daniel the Fourth Man in "Life's Fiery Furnaces."

Who is this Fourth Man?

In Hosea, he is the Faithful Husband, "Forever married to the backslider."

In Joel, he is the Baptizer with the Holy Ghost and Fire.

In Amos, he is our Burden-Bearer.

In Obadiah, he is the Mighty to Save.

In Jonah, he is our great Foreign Missionary.

In Micah, he is the Messenger of Beautiful Feet.

In Nahum, he is the Avenger of God's Elect.

In Habakkuk, he is God's Evangelist, crying, "Revive the work in the midst of the years."

In Zephaniah, he is our Savior.

In Haggai, he is the Restorer of God's Lost Heritage.

In Zechariah, he is the Fountain opened up in the

House of David for Sin and Uncleanness.

In Malachi, he is the Sun of Righteousness, rising with Healing in his Wings.

Who is this fourth Man?

In Matthew, he is the Messiah.

In Mark, he is the Wonder Worker.

In Luke, he is the Son of Man.

In John, he is the Son of God.

In Acts, he is the Holy Ghost.

In Romans, he is our Justifier.

In 1 and 2 Corinthians, he is our Sanctifier.

In Galatians, he is our Redeemer from the Curse of the Law.

In Ephesians, he is the Christ of Unsearchable Riches.

In Philippians, he is the God who Supplies all our Needs.

In Colossians, he is the Fullness of the Godhead Bodily.

In 1 and 2 Thessalonians, he is our Soon Coming King.

In 1 and 2 Timothy, he is our Mediator between God and Man.

In Titus, he is our Faithful Pastor.

In Philemon, he is a Friend that sticketh closer than a brother.

Who is this Fourth Man?

In Hebrews, he is the Blood of the Everlasting Covenant.

In James, he is our Great Physician, for "The prayer of faith shall save the sick."

In 1 and 2 Peter, he is our Chief Shepherd "Who shall soon appear with a Crown of Unfading Glory.

In 1, 2, and 3 John, he is Love.

In Jude, he is the Lord coming with ten thousands of his Saints.

And in Revelation, he is the King of Kings and the Lord of Lords!"[1]

THE ANGEL IN PRISON

I love where the writer of Hebrews declares, *"And what shall I more say?"* (Hebrews 11:32) God is so good that you can't tell it all. The good things he has done since Christ came to help all of mankind return to the Father.

The gift of faith brings courage and supernatural peace in times of danger and crisis. It is *"the peace of God, which passeth all understanding, shall keep your hearts and minds through Christ Jesus* (Philippians 4:7).

What would be your response if you were told, "Tomorrow you will die"?

---

1. Roberts, Oral, *The Fourth Man*, Standard Printing Co. Print.

I am sure to Peter this was not an empty threat. Herod had just killed James, the brother of John. Then he had Peter arrested and kept in prison (Acts 12:2-4). The church began to pray without ceasing. Sometimes I wonder what it will take to get some folks to start praying. They had just killed James, but when Peter was arrested, they began to pray.

What does Peter do the night he faces execution? He was sleeping between two soldiers. He was chained and behind closed doors. Sleeping! Then an angel came to deliver him from the prison.

> **And, behold, the ANGEL OF THE LORD came upon him, and a light shined in the prison: and he smote Peter on the side, and raised him up, saying, Arise up quickly. And his chains fell off from his hands.**
>
> **Acts 12:7**

Peter had a word from Jesus that helped him to believe even in prison, chained to two soldiers. *"But when thou shalt be old, thou shalt stretch forth thy hands, and another shall gird thee, and carry thee whither thou wouldest not* (John 21:18). Speaking of his crucifixion and not beheading as they had done to James. This is a supernatural peace that provided him courage in the time of crisis.

JESUS HELPED US IN JAMAICA

Andrew DeRier and I had just landed at the Norman Manley Airport in Kingston, Jamaica. Our flight from New York City had been delayed. We arrived in the country in the early evening.

When we went to get our passports stamped and visa papers signed, the customs agent told us that he was deporting us and sending us back to New York. When I asked him why he answered, "You are CIA agents!"

I told him jokingly that I couldn't spell CIA. He didn't think that it was funny, and we were escorted to the airport holding cell. When they shut the cell door and walked away, peace came on me, and I believed that we would stay and preach the meeting.

I grabbed the cell door and shook it, and when I did, it came open! So I went out into the corridor and walked down the hall and back out into the airport terminal. When the agent saw me, his eyes got big. Before he could speak, I said, "God told me to come to Jamaica and preach. I know you think that I am a CIA agent, but I am a Holy Ghost preacher, and if you are the only one I preached to, here it goes."

He said, "Hold on! I am a backslidden New Testament Church of God." He stamped our passports but gave us extra days on our visas which we needed because the meetings were extended, and we saw hundreds saved. I know that strong belief was the gift of faith that day.

THE ANGEL IN THE STORM

The apostle Paul was under arrest and being transported to Rome to stand before Caesar. They sailed towards the island of Crete and came up under the island near Fair havens, the southernmost point.

Paul received a word from the Lord concerning the ship's destruction and their lives. *"I perceive that this voyage will be with hurt and much damage, not only of the lading and ship, but also of our lives"* (Acts 27:10).

We learn later that the gift of faith proved to be greater than this revelation gift Paul was operating in at that time. Something changed between what he told them in Acts 27:10 and what he then said:

> **And now I exhort you to be of good cheer: for there shall be no loss of any man's life among you, but of the ship.**
> **Acts 27:22**

I find this as another evident proof that the gift of faith is greater in operation than this particular revelation gift.

Again an angel is present in bringing this message to Paul in the storm (Acts 27:23). Paul did nothing but believe God.

> **Wherefore, sirs, be of good cheer: FOR I BELIEVE GOD, that it shall be even as it was told me.**
> **Acts 27:25**

They ate and then cast the wheat into the sea. There was talk of killing the prisoners, but the centurion wanted to spare Paul. The devil wants to kill you in the storms of life, but the Lord has a plan for your deliverance and safety.

The ship ran aground and began to break up. Then the men jumped into the stormy water *"and the rest, some on boards, and some on broken pieces of the ship. And so it came to pass, that they escaped all safe to land"* (Acts 27:44).

God can take those things which seem broken in your life, and he can use them to bring you to safety.

Broken boards and pieces became vehicles of deliverance to the shore of safety (Acts 27:44).

Broken bread becomes healing for the sick body (1 Corinthians 11:24).

Broken pitchers became the light of deliverance for Gideon's band. (Judges 7:19)

You're going to make it!

The bills are piling up, and you're facing bankruptcy . . . you're going to make it.

The doctors have given up hope on your loved ones . . . you're going to make it.

The days look dark, and the storms of life are raging . . . you're going to make it.

The children are not serving the Lord . . . they are going to make it.

CHAPTER 5
Living in the Overflow

There is a song we used to sing in First Assembly in Harrisburg when I was growing up. I can still see Brother Schambach's sister, Margaret, on the front row, hands raised with tears flowing down her cheeks. Grace on the organ and the saints singing to the Lord. The song was called *"God Will Take Care of You."*

First Verse
Be not dismayed Whate'er betide,
God will take care of you;
Beneath His wings of love abide,
God will take care of you.
Chorus
God will take care of you,
Through ev'ry day, o'er all the way;
He will take care of you,

God will take care of you.
Second Verse
Through days of toil when heart doth fail,
God will take care of you;
When dangers fierce your path assail,
God will take care of you.
Third Verse
No matter what may be the test,
God will take care of you;
Lean, weary one, upon His breast,
God will take care of you.

Margaret and her brother Jim were my Sunday school teachers growing up. They taught us stories of how God took care of his children, which produced a trust in my heart that everything was always going to be alright. I was learning about the gift of faith before I even knew there was a gift of faith.

THE GIFT OF FAITH AND SUPERNATURAL PROVISION

One of the characteristics of the gift of faith is that there is supernatural provision for God's children. The story of Elijah at the brook Cherith is a great example of how the gift of faith worked in providing sustenance for the prophet of God.

> And the WORD OF THE LORD came unto him, saying, Get thee hence, and turn thee eastward, and hide thyself by the brook Cherith that is before Jordan. And it shall be that thou shalt drink of the brook; and I HAVE COMMANDED THE RAVENS TO FEED THEE THERE. So he went and did according unto the word of the Lord: for he went and dwelt by the brook Cherith that is before Jordan. And the ravens brought him bread and flesh in the morning, and bread and flesh in the evening; and he drank of the brook.
> 1 Kings 17:2-6

The raven was considered an unclean bird. The story of Noah gives us insight into how the raven went out but never came back.

> And he sent forth A RAVEN, which went forth to and fro, until the waters were dried up from off the earth. Also he sent forth a dove from him, to see

> if the waters were abated from off the face of the ground; But the dove found no rest for the sole of her foot, and she returned unto him into the ark, for the waters were on the face of the whole earth: then he put forth his hand, and took her, and pulled her in unto him into the ark.
>
> **Genesis 8:7-9**

In his commentary, Matthew Henry thought that the raven had found a floating carcass to rest upon and feed.[1] The raven did not return to the ark, so Noah sent forth a dove which returned until the land was dry, and then it flew away.

The contrast between the flood waters and the brook of Cherith, which dried up, is interesting to me. Water is the source of life. The Word of Almighty God produced the flood, and that same word brought a drought.

> **And Elijah the Tishbite, who was of the inhabitants of Gilead, said unto Ahab, As the Lord God of Israel liveth, before**

---

1. See Matthew Henry's Concise Commentary on Genesis 8:4-12

whom I stand, THERE SHALL NOT BE DEW NOR RAIN THESE YEARS, but according to my word.

       1 Kings 17:1

The brook speaks of the *prophetic* word, and the ravens speak of the *provision* of the word. That supernatural provision was Elijah operating in the gift of faith. He did nothing but *receive*.

I read that the ravens were bringing the prophet food from Ahab's table. Jewish tradition speaks of two trained ravens that were perched at the royal table of the King of Judah.[2] All that Elijah had to do was *receive*. The gift of faith produces the best.

God is a God of more than enough!

Elijah at the brook Cherith was the operation of the gift of faith. Elijah at Zarephath was the operation of the working of miracles.

When the brook finally dried up, the Lord led his servant to a widow where he had food by the working of miracles. There was a widow woman in Zarephath that was out gathering sticks to build a fire. When Elijah saw her, he asked her to get him water to drink. As

---

2. Mindel, Nissan. "Elijah the Prophet." Chabad.Org, www.chabad.org/library/article_cdo/aid/111833/jewish/Elijah-the-Prophet.htm.

she went to fetch the water, he asked her for bread.

> **As the Lord thy God liveth, I have not a cake, but an handful of meal in a barrel, and a little oil in a cruse: and, behold, I am gathering two sticks, that I may go in and dress it for me and my son, that we may eat it, and die.**
>
> **1 Kings 17:12**

What a powerful truth from God's Word. Here is a paradox, *if you eat it, you will die, but if you give it, you will live.* When we obey the Word of the Lord, we can expect an overflow of provision. The miracle lasted until the day that the rains returned.

> **And the barrel of meal wasted not, neither did the cruse of oil fail, according to the word of the Lord, which he spake by Elijah.**
>
> **1 Kings 17:16**

We are reminded to *"Believe in the Lord your God, so shall ye be established; believe his prophets, so shall ye prosper."* (2 Chronicles 20:20)

The Israelites lived *in the overflow*. (Exodus 16)

The widow of Zarephath lived *in the overflow*. (1 Kings 17:16)

The 5,000 lived *in the overflow*. (John 6)

The widow of one of the sons of the prophets lived *in the overflow*. (2 Kings 4:1-7)

The nation of Israel *received* supernatural provision in the wilderness. (Exodus 16:15; Numbers 11:31; Numbers 20:11.) They did nothing to produce it but *received* it daily for forty years.

THE GIFT OF FAITH FEEDS THE FIVE THOUSAND

> **When Jesus then lifted up his eyes, and saw a great company come unto him, he saith unto Philip, Whence shall we buy bread that these may eat? And this he said to prove him: FOR HE HIMSELF KNEW WHAT HE WOULD DO.**
>
> **John 6:5, 6**

He already knew what he would do *before* the miracle of the multiplying of the loaves and fishes. Jesus fed the five thousand by the gift of faith. (John 6:6) It is interesting that the Lord tested Philip for his response.

> **One of his disciples, Andrew, Simon Peter's brother, saith unto him, there is a lad here, which hath FIVE BARLEY LOAVES, AND TWO SMALL FISHES: but what are they among so many?**
>
> **John 6:8, 9**

Somehow our precious Lord takes what we have and turns it into what we need. A tremendous crowd had followed him. Christ's concern was to provide for those who followed him. The gift of faith is activated by the challenge of provision. It then released supernatural provision.

You get what you sow. The Lord took these loaves and fishes, and they were multiplied by God's power of multiplication and increase. We are reminded of the law of sowing and reaping found in Genesis 8:22. *"While the earth remaineth, SEEDTIME AND HARVEST, and cold and heat, and summer and winter, and day and night shall not cease."*

That boy's lunch was the seed for the miracle harvest of five thousand lunches.

I have studied the kinds of prayer in the Bible. When we examine how Jesus prayed in this story, there are two interesting things that we must examine. Jesus blessed or prayed over the bread, whereas he divided or gave out of the fish. (John 6:11)

Notice how Mark records this moment.

> **And when he had taken the five loaves and the two fishes, he looked up to heaven, and BLESSED, AND BRAKE THE LOAVES, and gave them to his disciples to set before them; and THE TWO FISHES DIVIDED HE among them all.**
>
> **Mark 6:41**

Jesus prayed a blessing over the bread. The fish, however, he cut up (divided) and gave them out. Why didn't he pray over the fish? The Bible indicates, *"For he himself knew what he would do"* (John 6:6).

We are reminded that the bread needed God's blessing because it was *made by man.*

The fish were divided up and given out as they were already blessed because *God made them.* (Genesis 1:21, 22)

The gift of faith gives access to the earthly realm and the heavenly realm.

The gift of faith is seen in these words, *"For he himself knew what he would do"* (John 6:6). This produced the miracle of the feeding of the five thousand. The gift of faith then produces an overflow.

> **When THEY WERE FILLED, he said unto his disciples, Gather up the fragments that remain, that nothing be lost. Therefore they gathered them together, AND FILLED TWELVE BASKETS with the fragments of the five barley loaves, which remained over and above unto them that had eaten.**
> John 6:12, 13

DAVID MACINTYRE

Our lives are shaped by the experiences we have and the people that the Lord sends to us. When I left Bible school to travel and evangelize, the Lord sent me, in February of 1977, to work with a mighty man of faith. His name was David MacIntyre.

When he was a boy, David was abandoned by his alcoholic father in the Canadian wilderness. His father took him and his brother to a trapper's cabin, then, in the early morning light, he abandoned them and left them to starve or freeze to death.

David took an axe and cut wood for the fire, and opened rusty cans filled with some food. They did not starve or freeze. He knew that they had to try and make it back to town, and the day came when they made it back, wading through the deep snow.

David told me he grew up angry and mean, and then the Gospel changed everything for him. He met Mary, and they got married. They answered the call of God and enrolled in Zion Bible Institute and, upon graduation, returned to New Brunswick. He and his wife, Mary, became the directors of Whited Bible Camp in 1967. He had two daughters, Karen and Kathy.

He pastored several churches in New Brunswick and in Maine, as well. I preached in two of them; the one in Hartland, New Brunswick, and the one just outside of Washburn, Maine. He first invited me up to preach in his church in Hartland, New Brunswick, in February 1977. What a great man he was, and he became like a father to me.

THE SECRET OF HIS POWER

Brother MacIntyre believed in operating in all of the nine gifts of the Spirit. When I stayed in his home that winter of 1977, I discovered his secret. He came and knocked on my bedroom door on one of the first mornings that I was there. "Let's go pray," he said.

It was 4:30 am! I thought that we would go downstairs by the stove to pray, but he grabbed his coat, and we headed out to the woodshed. There was a large stump with over a hundred rings on it. Those rings represented each year of the tree's life until it was cut down.

That stump became our daily altar. I prayed loud and strong to keep warm. Every day the Holy Spirit would make his presence felt. Brother Mac told me, "If you pray every day until the anointing comes on you, then you will never backslide." Fresh fire!

Then the Lord would show him something to do for that morning or day, or even the week. We would then go and do it. Supernatural revelation comes from the anointing of the Spirit.

Brother Mac taught me that whatever the Lord shows you to do, then he is responsible to provide for that assignment. Supernatural provision comes from obedience to the heavenly vision. Where God guides, he provides, and where he leads, he will feed.

GOD IS YOUR SOURCE

The MacIntyres gave their entire ministry to the camp, and it grew in the 60s and 70s. It was busting at the seams by the 80s. Dormitories had to be built, and expansion was needed to handle the hundreds of young men and women who were coming.

Brother MacIntyre told me that the day came when he knew the churches would not always help him. When he took over the Whited Bible Camp, the Lord began to bless the youth ministry until he had the largest youth camp in New England.

He needed resources to build and expand, but the money was in limited supply. There was a need for new dormitories. He needed steel to carry the heavy snow loads in the winter. The cost seemed prohibitive, and no one had the burden, but he had the assignment, and he told me it was up to God to provide it.

He lived across the border in Waterville next to the Trans-Canada Highway. The Lord began to wake him up in the winter and led him to go up on the Trans-Canada and pray. One morning, the Lord told him to call in the steel by the gift of faith.

He went to the same spot every morning and called in the steel for the camp. He told me that he would look over the snow-covered field on the other side of the road and thank God for the steel. He did that throughout the winter until spring began to melt the snow.

One morning he looked and saw a dark shape sticking up through the melting snow. When he went to investigate, it was a load of steel that had been buried under the snow. He contacted the New Brunswick Provincial Police (NBPP), and they got ahold of the RCMP in Ottawa.

There was no claim by any trucking company for the steel, so Brother Mac got a friend to bring a flatbed over, and they hoisted the steel up on the truck bed. With no customs fee to pay, they brought it over to the camp.

When they measured the steel and figured out the cuts, it was exactly the dimensions needed to build the dormitory! The gift of faith put him into the steel business. I always shout when I remember this great source of supply from our heavenly Father.

THE GIFT OF FAITH FOR FOOD

One day, we were working at the camp, and it was lunchtime. We went up to Smith's truck stop to eat. I did not have any money, nor did he. Brother Mac told me we would trust God to receive our food. What did that mean? He ordered a huge meal, and I ordered a glass of water.

We ate, and then it came time to pay the bill. He looked at me and laughed. He said, "We have worked all morning for the Lord, and he is responsible to take care of the meal."

We sat there for a few minutes when an elderly lady came by the table and spoke to Brother Mac about how much she appreciated him holding the funeral for her sister. Then picking up the bill, she walked to the register. He left full, but I left hungry.

"Well, what are you getting?" We were back the next day, and he was ordering. We still had no money, so I ordered water, and he had a turkey dinner. He was laughing at me. He thought I was fasting. Again he ate, and then while we were sitting there, a man called Royce Sargent came by the table and talked with Brother Mac, then he took the bill!

On the third day, we went back, and I ordered a double Smith burger with fries and a soda. He sat there with a twinkle in his eye, just laughing. Today was different; no one came by the table. I thought, "We are washing dishes to cover the bill."

We sat there, and he pumped faith into my heart. Forty-five minutes went by, and we were talking when our waitress Sherry came and said you can leave anytime you want; someone paid your bill! We had *received* and did not know it.

The gift of faith receives supernatural provision. You *believe* God and take him at his Word. I have often thought that all blessings that we receive come from the hand of God. The gift of faith produces that provision at the moment of need. It is always on time and never late.

THE GIFT OF FAITH CAN BE IMPARTED TO ANOTHER

One of the stories where the gift of faith combines both supernatural courage in the time of crisis and supernatural provision in times of great need is the story of the widow in 2 Kings 4.

> **Now there cried a certain woman of the wives of the sons of the prophets unto Elisha, saying, Thy servant my husband is dead; and thou knowest that thy servant did fear the Lord: and the creditor is come to take unto him my two sons to be bondmen.**
> **2 Kings 4:1**

Her husband had died. He had been a part of the company known as the *"sons of the prophets."* His unfortunate death left his wife and two sons in serious debt. Those to whom he owed money were coming to take her two sons into bondage. They would have to work off their father's debt. Her debt was destroying the home.

Her heart is broken by the loss of her husband, and the burden was compounded by the removal of her two sons from the home. She then went to Elisha for help in this present crisis. *"Believe in the Lord your God, so shall ye be established; believe his prophets, SO SHALL YE PROSPER."* (2 Chronicles 20:20)

This was her impartation from the man of God.

> **And Elisha said unto her, WHAT SHALL I DO FOR THEE? tell me, what hast thou in the house? And she said, Thine handmaid hath not anything in the house, SAVE A POT OF OIL.**
>
> **2 Kings 4:2**

It would seem her statement contradicted itself. *"I don't have anything, but I do have something."* I believe that Elisha stimulated her belief, and at that moment, nothing became something. Her answer became her miracle.

She was not *double-minded* because she did receive her miracle. We know that the Scripture states:

> **But let him ask in faith, nothing wavering. For he that wavereth is like a wave**

> of the sea driven with the wind and tossed. For let not that man think that he shall receive anything of the Lord. A double-minded man is unstable in all his ways.
>
> **James 1:6-8**

I believe at that moment, she got infected with Elisha's spirit. The gift of faith came alive in her because of what Elisha said, and it was at that moment everything changed. He then gave her instructions to set her up for a miracle.

EMPTY VESSELS (that's their condition).

> Then he said, Go, borrow thee vessels abroad of all thy neighbors, even empty vessels, BORROW NOT A FEW.
>
> **2 Kings 4:3**

The gift of faith immediately becomes greater than your challenge or crisis. I want you to notice that the focus has now shifted from the pot of oil (that is the supply) to the vessels. There was no limit as to what she could borrow.

It senses an overflow is coming. It is something bigger than your natural circumstances can confine you to. You believe, at that moment, what you are about to receive will far outweigh your limitations.

We expect a miracle!

VESSELS ABROAD (that's their location).

The man of God told her to go out of her house because there were not enough in the house. She then would determine the size of her blessing. The vessels were all around her "abroad," but their location was about to change. Where you are is not where you are going to finish. There was a place where the miracle would begin. God will bring you to that place where he can bless you.

The gift of faith denies lack and receives an overflow!

> **So she went from him, and shut the door upon her and upon her sons, who brought the vessels to her and she POURED out.**
>
> **2 Kings 4:5**

VESSELS THAT ARE FULL (that is her expectation).

> **And it came to pass, when the vessels were full, that she said unto her son, Bring me yet a vessel, And he said unto**

> her, There is not a vessel more. A n d the oil stayed. Then she came and told the man of God. And he said, Go sell the oil, and pay thy DEBT, and live thou and thy children of the rest.
>
> 2 Kings 4:6, 7

The oil kept flowing until there were no more vessels to fill. Her blessing was determined by her expectation. The gift of faith took her from empty to full.

The miracle came after she *believed* the word of the Lord. There was an overflow because the miracle oil paid off her debt, and there was enough for her and her two sons to live on the rest.

There is so much in this incredible story of faith, but the great lesson is that you can *receive* the operation of God's Spirit from the impartation and instruction of another.

The gift of faith aids in supernatural provision.

The gift of faith transferred the covenant blessings from the Old Testament patriarchs to their sons. It is seen in Isaac laying his hands upon Jacob and pronouncing the blessing upon him (Genesis 27:27-29).

The apostle Paul encouraged his son in the Gospel to stir up the gift that was in him by the laying on of his hands (2 Timothy 1:6). Then we are reminded of Paul's words, *"For I long to see you, that I may impart unto you some spiritual gift, to the end ye may be established"* (Romans 1:11).

All blessings and gifts come from God's Spirit. He chooses to use men and women as conduits of his grace and power.

THE GIFT OF FAITH FOR FINANCES

The Lord dealt with me in the early days of my ministry about finances. I had read Gordon Lindsay's book, *The Pentecostal Ministry*, and there was a chapter on the evangelist and the handling of finances. It really helped me in the early days.

During those first years of ministry, I never knew how much money I would have or even if there would be any money. At one meeting, they gave me a ham, a jar of green beans, and a dozen eggs. When I came home to my father's house, he must have known I was feeling down, and he asked how much the offering was.

When I told him, he jumped up and said, "Good, we are going to eat your offering!" My mom came downstairs, and it was late. Dad told her to make biscuits. We sat around the table eating ham and eggs and warm biscuits. I felt better.

When I started out, it was unheard of for any minister to have financial requirements. You just preached and ministered freely. Pastors were not looking for package benefits for retirement and financial security. Evangelists just went, and pastors just preached.

Missionaries who may have stood as apostles, teachers, pastors, or evangelists in other nations received support from churches in their denominations so that they could remain on the field for extended lengths of time. There were some who did not have any backing, but the Lord took care of them.

I have watched the spirit of corruption (Mammon) come into the modern-day Church. Revivals were turned into fundraisers. Traveling ministries began to set fees, and there were some who charged for prayer. Churches gave honorariums, themselves setting fees, like secular companies that bring in motivational speakers.

One evangelist went into a town and rented an auditorium, and told the crowd that everyone that would give $100 would be healed the rest of their lives.

A pastor told a large crowd that there was a "millionaire" anointing in his meeting, and the first one thousand people to come down and give $1000 dollars that God would make them millionaires.

When we were in New Jersey, my wife was told that

the crowd was shocked that I prayed and prophesied over the people for free. There were so-called prophets charging the people for prayer and prophecies for exorbitant amounts of money in that area.

These ungodly ministers will go to hell just like Korah and his followers did if they don't repent. Jesus gave only ONE requirement to his first ministers, do not bother to have money, food, or extra clothing; just GO!

> **Then he called his twelve disciples together, and gave them power and authority over all devils, and to cure diseases. And he sent them to preach the kingdom of God, and to heal the sick. And he said unto them, TAKE NOTHING for your journey, neither staves, or scrip, neither bread, neither money; neither have two coats apiece. And whatsoever house ye enter into, there abide, and thence depart.**
> **Luke 9:1-4**

The first thing that Jesus did was to give his followers an anointing to deal with devils and diseases and promised to back them with the authority of the kingdom of God as they went out to preach.

WHAT THE LORD TOLD ME ABOUT MONEY

The day came when the Lord spoke to me about money. I was fasting and praying for notable miracles to take place in the meetings and, in particular, for the blind to see; when I heard these words, "Which is greater souls or money?"

I was shocked. Did the Lord think I was in the ministry for money? If I was, where was it? Then he spoke those words to me a second time, "Which is greater, souls or money?"

I bowed myself and continued to pray and fast when he spoke a third time, "Which is greater, souls or money?" Then I heard, "If you don't have faith for the lesser, which is money, how will you have faith for the greater, which are souls?"

> **For what is man profited, if he shall gain the whole world, and lose his own soul? Or what shall a man give in exchange for his soul?**
> **Matthew 16:26**

I learned ONE SOUL is worth more than the combined wealth of the world! God is able to finance all of our efforts and work to bring in the end-time harvest. There is provision for the heavenly vision.

HOW TO BELIEVE FOR THE OVERFLOW

Then the Lord began to teach me about the gift of faith for finances. I was in Knoxville, Tennessee holding a meeting and was reading a teaching by a minister. He spoke about finances. He would get an amount he needed for the week and then call it in. Command the devil to take his hands off the money and loose angels to bring it in.

I believed that I would receive my money the same way that the Lord did for that minister. I needed $1000 that week. When I asked the pastor to agree with me, he told me that the most his church had ever given was $400. He told me I would have to believe for myself as he didn't think it would come in.

We said little or nothing about the offering and just received it from the dear folks each night. The last night he came into the back office upset. My first thought was, "Well, we must not have received it." He told me that the offering was over $1000! The Lord told me this was the gift of faith.

Angels brought food to Elijah, and they brought finances to me. I followed this procedure from then until today. When I did not have that knowing, I didn't receive an offering. When it comes on me, the money comes in, and many times I know how much before the count is finished.

Forty-six years of ministry have come and gone, and we are covering the world with the Gospel, and the ministry is debt-free. Thank you, Jesus!

Remember, the two quickest judgments in the Bible had to do with the handling of money and possessions. Korah (Numbers 16:32) and his followers, and Ananias (Acts 5:3-5) and Sapphira (Acts 5:10).

Although some may think it extreme, the apostle John instructed the Church to set aside monies to support traveling ministers. Diotrephes opposed this plan, and John said that this was evil. (3 John 11) Demetrius gave a good report concerning this matter to all men. (3 John 12) It is a good thing for a church or people to use their money for the purpose of spreading the Gospel.

Pastors, please use this as a Bible example and become generous to traveling ministries. You that are traveling ministries receive your offerings each service and trust God for your finances. Make no demands but let the gift of faith help you to accomplish this.

It is always better to trust God. When the challenges

arise, and they do, the gift of faith works at that moment for supernatural provision.

THE GIFT OF FAITH TOOK ME AROUND THE WORLD

I set out to fly around the world to preach the Gospel when I was twenty-five years old. It all started in the fall of 1980 when I was preaching in North Carolina. There were several churches that came together for what they called a sectional rally. The meetings were conducted in Askewville at the Assembly of God church.

The day speaker was Brother Y. Jeyaraj, the general superintendent of the Assemblies of God in India. That night when I was done preaching, he said to me, "You must come to India next year!"

A few months later, Evangelist David Grant, who ministered in India, called me and encouraged me to come. He told me that he was going to help me with meetings there as well.

I had a crisis, I was invited to preach in India, but I did not have the money to go. I had 90 days to raise the $2,000 dollars. I had $2,500 come in the first year of ministry. Then from 1977 through 1980, I never had more than $5,000 come in. My faith was being stretched.

FRANK SUMRALL TAUGHT ME A GREAT LESSON

That fall, I was ministering in South Bend and went out to eat with Frank Sumrall. I told him of my need and what I believed for. I told him, "If I get the money, then I will go." His sweet rebuke changed my faith. "IF is the badge of doubt!" He told me, "Say, 'WHEN I get the money, I am going to preach in India.'"

That was the moment that the gift of faith came into my spirit. I knew I would have the money and would preach in India. Until that time, I never had more than $5,000 dollars come in a year, but now I was setting my faith for $2,000 dollars to come in two months' time.

January came, and I was sitting in the lounge of Pan American Airlines in New York City. The Lord helped me to get an around-the-world ticket on the Pan Am Clipper. I had $37 dollars in my pocket. I had no credit card in those days. There were $400 dollars of travelers' checks I had set aside in my coat pocket.

"Do you have rupee?" An Indian gentleman sitting next to me asked. I thought he meant a sickness or physical condition. Before I could answer, he said, "What do you do?" I told him that I was flying to India to preach faith to the people and pray for the sick.

Tears came into his eyes. He told me that he was a

Hindu. Then he invited me into the restaurant there and bought my supper. Those airport prices were high. He said, "Order what you want; I will pay." I got a steak and potato and an apple ring. I shared Christ with him, and the Lord anointed us.

When we went back out to the lounge, he asked me again, "Do you have rupee?" Then he proceeded to pull money from his pocket and stuff it into mine. He saw a man from his country and told him of my mission and then asked the man to give me rupees. I had two coat pockets full!

That seventeen-hour flight took me to Bombay (Mumbai). I did not know there was an entry tax. I pulled out the rupees and had more than enough to pay the fee.

God blessed me on that trip. One day, God asked me to give the travelers' checks to a widow that ran a Christian school and church. Then, it was a minister's birthday, and he got what I had. Oh, the glorious gift of faith.

Then it was on to Hong Kong and Tokyo, and I blessed the missionaries there. Now I was ready to fly home, and I found out that my flight was overbooked and I was grounded in the Tokyo airport.

David, an employee of Northwest Orient, handed me a plastic standby card with the number one on it.

He asked me if he could order a meal. I ordered a steak and potato, and they brought an apple ring.

I then began to walk and pray when that gift of faith kicked in! I knew that I was flying out that day. So I sat down to wait when a young girl came and sat down next to me and began to cry. When I asked her what was wrong, she told me that she had been bumped from the flight.

Then she said, "The standby pass is not available, so I may be here until next week." That pass was in my pocket. The Lord said to me, "You believe that you're flying out today, so give her the pass." I gave it to her. David ran from behind the desk, yelling at me, "No more food, no more pass."

The girl was a missionary to Taiwan headed home to America. She was happy to have the pass. A seat became available on the Northwest Orient flight to Honolulu. She got up and waved and went down the runway. When David came back, he gave me a look of disdain.

I said to him, "David, Jesus told me that I would leave here today." He told me that he was a Buddhist and did not believe in Jesus. No sooner had he said that when his walkie-talkie came on, and he listened and then said, "Follow me."

Korean Airlines had a seat in first class, and it was

the last flight of the day. David said as I boarded, "Jesus got you a seat." The stewardess came and gave me the choice of steak or lobster. I ordered both! When I landed in Honolulu and went to clear customs, I heard a girl behind me call my name. It was the missionary from Taiwan. I had beaten her to Hawaii.

The gift of faith took me around the world!

It is released by the Holy Spirit's ministry.

It is God revealing Himself at the point of our receiving.

The gift of faith makes the impossible possible!

...The blind see, the lame walk, the lepers are cleansed, the deaf hear, the dead are raised, to the poor the Gospel is preached.

Luke 7:22

CHAPTER 6

The Gift of Faith: An Instrument of Dominion

The gift of faith is activated in times of trouble and danger. The gift of faith takes over when you have used up the faith that you have as a believer. It is Heaven's reserve tank that never runs dry!

The gift of faith and all of the gifts of the Spirit work by *"that one and selfsame Spirit"* (1 Corinthians 12:11). He is always willing to use us for the deliverance of humanity. The gifts, therefore, are the antidote to the work of Satan and evil spirits. They are our weapons for victory.

> **For the weapons of our warfare are not carnal, but mighty through God to the pulling down of strong holds;**
> **2 Corinthians 10:4**

There are four operations of the gift of faith that I would like to examine in this study:

- Casting out of devils (Mark 16:17).
- Raising the dead (Matthew 10:8).
- Supernatural transportation (Acts 8:39, 40).
- Transfer of the anointing or impartation (Romans 1:11).

1. Casting out of devils

I will go into greater detail about the casting out of devils more than the other operations, as it was a part of the Great Commission for world evangelization and soul-winning (Mark 16:15, 16). and is one of the four signs that confirm the Word (Mark 16:17, 18).

THE DEVIL WENT TO BIBLE SCHOOL

East Providence, Rhode Island, was the home of Zion Bible Institute, where I went to Bible School. One night, after class, when my friends and I came out of Gracemore A (one of our classrooms), we heard people yelling across the street. We saw a young man swinging a leather belt and threatening the church folks who had come out of the building.

We ran across the street to help the people, and the young man took off running. I took off after him and chased him around the church and back into the parking lot, then towards the school library. A haze began to cover his head, and he said, "I am going to kill you tonight!" That was the night I came face to face with a demon-possessed man.

We found out later that he professed to be a warlock and had brought two young girls that thought they were witches to disrupt the Bible study class. The police had been called, and they came and arrested them.

Since I was a student, an instructor told me to go to my dorm room. I went to bed. Sometime in the night, I woke up sweating, and my body was trembling. When I looked up, there was a tall, dark shape standing at the foot of my bed. I was in the top bunk.

My roommate, Sterling, woke up at that moment and said, "I rebuke you, Satan, in Jesus' name!" I saw that shape go right out the window. Later, I asked Sterling if he had seen the shape. He told me he hadn't seen it but had felt an evil spirit.

Since that time, the Lord has allowed me to cast out devils here in America and in Canada, Mexico, the West Indies, Europe, Scandinavia, India, and Africa. The Devil has nowhere to hide, and the Gospel light shines brightly around the world.

THE GIFT OF FAITH DEALS WITH THE DEVIL

Paul's prayer in 1 Thessalonians 5:23 reveals the threefold nature of man.

> **And the very God of peace sanctify you wholly; and I pray God your whole spirit and soul and body be preserved blameless unto the coming of our Lord Jesus Christ.**
>
> **1 Thessalonians 5:23**

How does God preserve us blameless? What does that mean? *"That he might present it to himself a glorious church, not having spot, or wrinkle, or any such thing; but that it should be holy and without blemish"* (Ephesians 5:27).

Paul reminds us that he is the *"very God of peace."*

There are three demon spirits that every believer will have to deal with.

The spirit of infirmity (Luke 13:11-13), which is your *body*.

The spirit of fear (2 Timothy 1:7), which is your *mind*.

The spirit of antichrist (1 John 4:3), which is your *spirit*.

Here is a beautiful plan of restoration for man. Your

body can be healed, your mind can be set free, and your spirit protected from the unrighteousness and filth of this present world.

The Lord spoke to a minister friend of mine that when he felt upset and irritated in his spirit but did not know why it was because "Your righteous spirit is rubbing up against the unrighteous spirit that is in the world." Thank God for the Holy Spirit and his wonderful gifts.

Our great God has provided the gifts of the Spirit to redeem fallen man and restore us to our rightful place in him. The gifts always operate in a redemptive context. The gift of faith in operation brings all of Heaven's resources to bear at that moment when a crisis or problem threatens the child of God.

When the enemy tries to rob the peace that God desires you to live in, there is divine protection for our spirit, soul, and body. We are made blameless by the Spirit of God through these supernatural gifts.

THE DEVIL WENT DOWN TO GEORGIA

My wife and I held one of our first revivals after we were married in Marietta, Georgia. It was in September of 1977. Pastor Albert Vickers and his wife graciously invited us to their church, and we stayed in the parsonage with them.

On the opening night, a woman started loudly screaming during the singing and praise. It was like a shriek of terror, and the Spirit seemed to lift off of the service. The woman came to the altar weeping and tormented. Sister Vickers and my wife knelt to pray with her, but it was like pouring gasoline on a fire. She screamed all the louder.

I bowed my head, asking the Lord to help the woman, when suddenly I saw her in a vision. She was dressed in black leather pants and a vest. She held a bottle of liquor in her hand and was lying on the seat of a motorcycle. The block building was painted orange and black.

Then I heard the sweet voice of the Lord in my spirit. "The devil is attacking her mind. He is reminding her of past sin. When you were singing about my Blood, a demon spirit began to accuse her."

A strong knowing and faith came up in my spirit, and I knew that I could set her free by the power of the Spirit. I went down and knelt next to her and began to tell her what the Lord showed me. She said, "Are you a psychic?" I told her that while she was singing, these thoughts attacked her mind.

She said that what I saw by the Holy Spirit were the exact images that came into her mind while she was singing. I remembered the verse, *"he cast out the spirits with his word"* (Matthew 8:16).

I knew at that moment that if I could speak a word from the Bible to her, she would be free. The Lord gave me this word:

> **There is therefore now no condemnation to them which are in Christ Jesus, who walk not after the flesh, but after the Spirit.**
>
> **Romans 8:1**

She instantly stopped crying and began to praise the Lord. I believe that the Lord gave me a *word of knowledge* and the *gift of faith* to bring healing and deliverance to the woman. Glory!

JESUS CAST OUT THE DEVILS

When we study the ministry of Jesus in the Gospels, we discover that one-third of the people he ministered to had a spirit that had to be dealt with before healing and deliverance could come.

- Jesus cast out devils, and the sick were then healed (Matthew 8:16).

- Jesus healed many with plagues caused by spirits (Mark 3:10, 11).
- Jesus preached, and those that had unclean spirits were healed (Luke 6:18).
- Jesus healed certain women who had evil spirits (Luke 8:2).
- Jesus healed a man who was blind and dumb caused by a devil (Matthew 12:22).
- Jesus set the insane free (Matthew 8:28-32; Mark 5:1-13; Luke 8:26-33).
- Jesus healed a deaf-mute by casting out the devil (Matthew 9:32, 33).
- Jesus sent his disciples to cast out devils, and many were healed (Mark 6:13).
- Jesus healed a mother's daughter that was vexed by a devil (Matthew 15:21-28).
- Jesus delivered a boy from mental illness by casting out a spirit (Matthew 17:18).
- Jesus healed a woman that was crippled by a spirit of infirmity (Luke 13:10-16).

When Jesus cast out devils, he was showing what his Father first did when the Father expelled Satan from Heaven. Since all faith is the nature of God manifested, then it had to be the gift of faith in operation in the ministry of Jesus in casting out devils.

It was not *saving faith* that brought this to pass, although every believer should be able to cast out devils (Mark 16:17). There are some who teach the devil will be saved. The devil will never be saved. In fact, he is destined for eternal punishment (Revelation 20:10).

It is not the daily walk of *general faith*. We are not casting devils out from morning to night, and neither did the Lord. Only one-third of Christ's miracles had to do with dealing with devils.

Certainly, it is not the *fruit of faith* or faithfulness that empowers us to cast out devils. The early disciples were instructed to cast out devils in the days immediately after their call. Any believer can cast out devils the moment they are saved.

Every believer, at some point, must understand that we are engaged in warfare. Paul reminds us, *"For we wrestle not against flesh and blood, but against principalities, against powers, against the rulers of the darkness of this world, against spiritual wickedness in high places."* (Ephesians 6:12). We must deal with the devil.

Our world needs deliverance. People deal with bondages and problems caused by demons. There are demons that operate as spirits of lust for alcohol, tobacco, and drugs; there are lying spirits; there are unclean spirits operating in sexual uncleanness and perversion. There seems to be a terrible spirit of violence and murder that is stalking our streets. Why?

In his book, "UNPROVOKED MURDER: Insanity or Demon Possession?" Dr. Sumrall wrote:

> It is clear that the responsibility for the problems of our times is not related solely to the courts and the judicial system, but part must be laid at the doorstep of the Church.
>
> In the Gospel of Mark, chapter 16:15-17, Jesus Christ said in the Great Commission to the Church: "Go ye into all the world, and preach the Gospel to every creature. He that believeth and is baptized shall be saved; but he that believeth not shall be damned. And these signs shall follow them that believe; In my name shall they cast out devils; . . ."
>
> According to these words of the Lord Jesus, anyone with the Spirit of God within him has the capability of relieving a person of a demon spirit through exorcism. According to 1 John 4:4, he that is in us is greater than he that is in the world. As Christians, we can truly set people free from the power of the devil.
>
> We cannot pass all the responsibility on to the judges and attorneys. The Church has a responsibility here. We must not fail this genera-

tion by being so cowardly that we will not face the issues of our time or the problems of our society."[1]

THE BATTLE OF THE AGES

Satan and his demons are real. The war between good and evil first began in Heaven, and then it came down to the Earth and was finished in Hell. The battle of the ages will culminate at the end of the millennium.

I believe that the rebellion of the Devil and fallen angels took place after the creation of the Earth because the Bible says, *"And God saw everything that he had made, and, behold, it was very good. And the evening and the morning were the sixth day"* (Genesis 1:31). Satan is not good nor the evil he does.

Isaiah records that Lucifer's downfall began in Heaven when God himself first cast the devil out. Isaiah gives us prophetic insight as to what led up to Satan's expulsion.

How art thou fallen from Heaven, O Lucifer, son of the morning! How art thou

---

[1]. Sumrall, Lester. "Chapter 8: Cultism and Unprovoked Murder." Unprovoked Murder: Is It Insanity or Demon Possession?, Harrison House, Tulsa, OK, 1981, pp. 120–121.

> cut down to the ground, which didst weaken the nations! For thou hast said in thine heart, I will ascend into Heaven, I will exalt my throne above the stars of God: I will sit also upon the mount of the congregation, in the sides of the north: I will ascend above the heights of the clouds; I will be LIKE the most High.
>
> **Isaiah 14:12-14**

What was the one thing the devil wanted but could never have? He said, *"I will be LIKE the most High"* (Verse 14). Our heavenly Father simply refused him, but instead, he said, *"Let us make man in our image, after our likeness:"* (Genesis 1:26). That is why the devil uses sicknesses and diseases, war and famine, and every evil thing to destroy mankind. We bear the image of God.

Our great God of Heaven cast the devil out first. Jesus said, *"And he said unto them, I beheld Satan as lightning fall from heaven"* (Luke 10:18).

God said, *"How art thou cut down to the ground (Earth) which didst weaken the nations"* (Isaiah 14:12). One translation records the word "weaken" as "make the nations sick."

> **Lucifer is not the counterpart of God, for God has no equal.**

The devil cannot win, will never win, and has never won. The downward spiral of Lucifer is seen in Scripture.

> **And the GREAT DRAGON was cast out, that old SERPENT, called the DEVIL, and SATAN, which deceiveth the whole world: he was cast out into the Earth, and his angels were cast out with him.**
>
> **Revelation 12:9**

We also know that one-third of the angels of Heaven fell with him and that they await their final judgment. The previous verse declares, *"And his tail drew THE THIRD PART OF THE STARS of heaven, and did cast them to the earth: and the dragon stood before the woman which was ready to be delivered, for to devour her child as soon as it was born"* (Revelation 12:4).

Contextually, in these verses, we see that the *"stars"* (Revelation 12:4) were Satan's *"angels"* (Revelation 12:9) that were cast out of Heaven. Then we see that those angels were cast down to hell.

> **For if God spared not the angels that sinned, but CAST THEM DOWN TO HELL, and delivered them into chains of darkness, to be reserved unto judgment;**
>
> **2 Peter 2:4**

> **And the angels which kept not their first estate, but left their own habitation, he hath reserved in everlasting chains under darkness unto the judgment of the great day.**
>
> **Jude 1:6**

The Scriptures indicate that the fallen angels have been consigned to hell waiting for that Judgment Day. Satan now resides in the Earth.

1. He can only be in one place at one time because he is not omnipresent.

The story of Job confirms that the Devil came down to Earth. *"And the Lord said unto Satan, Whence comest thou? Then Satan answered the Lord, and said, From going to and fro in the earth, and from walking up and down in it"* (Job 1:7).

2. *He only knows what you tell him, as he is not omniscient.*

The devil does not know everything. He is limited in his knowledge.

The devil did not know who Jesus was. *"And when the tempter came to him, he said, IF THOU BE THE SON OF GOD, command that these stones be made bread"* (Matthew 4:3).

Paul wrote, *"which none of the princes of this world knew: for had they known it, they would not have crucified the Lord of glory"* (1 Corinthians 2:8).

3. *He cannot overrule your will or determine your destiny. He is not omnipotent.*

The Devil has no power over the child of God. Jesus stripped him of his power on the Cross. Then Jesus declared, *"All power is given unto me in heaven and in earth"* (Matthew 28:18).

> **And they overcame him by the blood of the Lamb and by the word of their testimony; and they loved not their lives unto the death.**
>
> **Revelation 12:11**

When we, in obedience to Christ's command cast out

devils, then we are enforcing the victory of the Cross!

> **And I say also unto thee, That thou art Peter, and upon this rock I will build my church; and THE GATES OF HELL SHALL NOT PREVAIL against it.**
>
> **Matthew 16:18**

DOMINION LOST AND REGAINED

When God created Adam, he gave him *dominion* over all the Earth and everything that was on the Earth (Genesis 2). He made a wife for him and assigned him the task of managing the garden.

It is here that the serpent enters the scene. Again Revelation 12:9 reminds us who this old serpent was; he is called Satan or the Devil. There is a passage of Scripture that we read *"Thou hast been in Eden the garden of God"* (Ezekiel 28:13).

We are introduced by Ezekiel to the *"prince of Tyrus"* (Ezekiel 28:2), and then the narrative shifts from a man (Verse 9) to an anointed cherub (Verse 14). The language of this prophecy is similar to Isaiah 14.

> **Thou wast perfect in thy ways from the day that thou wast created, till iniquity**

was found in thee.

> Ezekiel 28:15

All they that know thee among the people shall be astonished at thee: thou shalt be a terror, and never shalt thou be any more.

> Ezekiel 28:19

Yet thou shalt be brought down to hell, to the sides of the pit. They that see thee shall narrowly look upon thee, and consider thee, saying, Is this the man that made the Earth to tremble, that did shake kingdoms;

> Isaiah 14:15, 16

The first attack against man's dominion was recorded in the Bible; it was wrapped in a lie that Satan told to Eve.

And the serpent said unto the woman, you shall not surely die:

> Genesis 3:4

When Eve believed the words of the serpent, and

Adam followed her by partaking of the forbidden fruit, that dominion was lost. *"For as by one man's disobedience many were made sinners, so by the obedience of one shall many be made righteous"* (Romans 5:19).

> **And Adam was not deceived, but the woman being deceived was in the transgression.**
>
> **1 Timothy 2:14**

Man's obedience to Satan's words brought death and sin. When a man receives God's Word, then the power of Satan is broken. Devils go when God's Word is declared.

> **When the even was come, they brought unto him many that were possessed with devils: and HE CAST OUT THE SPIRITS WITH HIS WORD, and healed all that were sick:**
>
> **Matthew 8:16**

The final and ultimate victory of Christ is seen in the netherworld of hell. What happened between the Cross and the Throne? Paul shows us by revelation that after Christ's death on the Cross, he descended into hell.

Now that he ascended, what is it but that he also descended first into the lower parts of the Earth?

Ephesians 4:9

Blotting out the handwriting of ordinances that was against us, which was contrary to us, and took it out of the way, nailing it to his Cross; and having SPOILED principalities and powers, he made a shew of them openly, TRIUMPHING over them in it.

Colossians 2:14, 15

Jesus took the dominion that was lost in the garden back. He "spoiled" these spirits of hell and victoriously triumphed over them. John the Revelator shows us this *"I am he that liveth, and was dead; and, behold, I am alive for evermore, Amen; and have the keys of hell and of death"* (Revelation 1:18).

When Jesus rose from the dead and began his ascension back to the Father, the Bible reveals that all those captive spirits that died in faith, *"These all died in faith, not having received the promises, but having seen them afar off, and were persuaded of them, and embraced them, and confessed that they were strangers and pilgrims on the earth"* (Hebrews 11:13) received their release after Christ's death and resurrection. Glory to God!

> **Wherefore he saith, when he ascended up on high, he led captivity captive, and gave gifts unto men.**
> **Ephesians 4:8**

What is man's greatest need?
What is the Devil's greatest problem?
What is God's greatest answer?

The answer is one person, JESUS! He is seen as the Lamb of God standing in the wings of time. When God the Father needed a deliverer to regain dominion, there was a great search for a man to open the book of God.

> **Who is worthy to open the book, and to loose the seals thereof? And no man in Heaven, nor in Earth, neither under the Earth, was able to open the book, neither to look thereon.**
> **Revelation 5:2-3**

It was a man that sold humanity out on the auction block of sin. When Adam surrendered his dominion to the Devil, it became the Devil's prize. Once God gave dominion to Adam, it was his to keep or lose. Adam gave it over to Satan, and now dominion over the Earth belonged to the evil one.

If God simply took the dominion back from Satan, He would have become a thief! The Father sought legal means to regain dominion. God's great search for a man began.

Jesus became the last Adam (1 Corinthians 15:45). He, the Lord Jesus, came to the Earth and lived his life without sin and then took back dominion by his sinless life, shed his blood for the covering of sin, and stripped all the power and dominion from the devil.

> **Wherefore God also hath highly exalted him, and given him a name which is above every name: that at the name of Jesus every knee should bow, of things in Heaven, and things in Earth, and things under the Earth;**
> **Philippians 2;9, 10**

When we cast out devils, we do so by the authority of what Jesus did. Satan is now a defeated foe. It is by the Holy Spirit that we are regaining the rightful place that was stolen from us.

The devil continually seeks to kill, steal, and destroy.

(John 10:10) He is like a roaring lion trying to devour what is yours (1 Peter 5:8). The gift of faith is in operation at this critical time of attack:

> **When the enemy shall come in like a flood, the Spirit of the Lord shall lift up a standard against him.**
> **Isaiah 59:19**

MY VISION OF THE STRONG MAN

The Lord gave me a vision when I was holding a meeting in Rowlett, Texas, in January of 2022. I saw this dark, fearsome creature appear on the right side of the auditorium in front of me. It seemed as tall as the ceiling.

I heard these words, "This is the strong man that is over America."

Then, a shaft of fire came down out of the ceiling, and it burned up the creature. When it did, then I saw the U.S. Capitol building was behind where the creature had stood. The Lord spoke to me, "This night, the strong man is destroyed."

Then I was caught up by the Spirit and carried over to the left side of the auditorium. There were bright flashing lights, and like a camera zooming in for the shot, I saw a sign that read Las Vegas.

Again I heard the Lord say, "In the city that people think I am least likely to move, I am sending a mighty revival. "Then the vision lifted, and I was standing in front of a young couple seated in the front row.

After the service, a minister I knew came to me and said that was my children you prophesied to, and they are leaving in the morning to go and start a church in Las Vegas.

It was this week that they announced the lock downs and masking would be extended. It did not happen! In March, they began to lift the mandates. I had an understanding that it was the Devil that tried to shut down and destroy America and the world, but God has the final say. I believe that the Lord used me for whatever reason to cast the strong man off of America that night.

We live in a fast-paced technological age, and many do not believe in devils or Satan. We must continue to cast out the devil at every opportunity.

THE EXPLODED DEVIL

> Men don't believe in a devil now, as their fathers used to do. They have opened the door of the widest creed to let his majesty through, and there isn't a print of his cloven foot, not a fiery

dart from his bow to be found in Earth or air today, for the world has voted it so.

But who is mixing the terrible draught that palsies the heart and brain?

Who loads the bier of each passing year with ten hundred thousand slain?

Who blights the bloom of the Earth today with the fiery breath of hell, if the devil isn't and never was, won't somebody rise and tell?

Who dogs the steps of the toiling saint? Who digs the pit for his feet?

Who sows the tares in the field of time wherever God sows the wheat?

The devil is voted not to be, and of course, the thing is true. But who is doing the terrible work which the devil alone should do?

We're told that he does not go about like a roaring lion now, but whom shall we hold responsible for the everlasting row to be heard in church and state today, to Earth's remotest bound, if the devil by unanimous vote is nowhere to be found?

Won't somebody step to the front forthwith and make his bow and show how the frauds and crimes of a single day spring up? We'd like to know.

The devil is voted not to be, and of course, the devil's gone, but simple people would like to know who carries his business on.[2]

2. Raising the Dead

The greatest confirmation that Christ reclaimed dominion is the resurrection of the dead. The apostle John heard these words on the isle of Patmos,

> **I am he that liveth, and was dead; and, behold, I am alive for evermore, Amen; and have the keys of HELL and of DEATH.**
> **Revelation 1:18**

JESUS RAISED THE DEAD IN HIS EARTHLY MINISTRY

There are three examples in the Bible of Jesus raising the dead. He raised a dead girl (Mark 5:42), a dead boy (Luke 7:15), and a dead friend (John 11:44). These three people were under the covenant that God made with

---

2. Alfred Hough, The Exploded Devil, POWER magazine, Volume 4; Number 11, October 1974, page 3

Abraham, just like the woman who had the spirit of infirmity in (Luke 13:16)

> **With LONG LIFE will I satisfy him, and shew him my salvation.**
> **Psalm 91:16**

This was a Psalm of Moses. It was not spoken by God's people but to God's people. The Midrash *(an ancient Jewish commentary)* states that Moses wrote this on the day that the building of the Tabernacle in the desert was finished.

Prior to the Cross but after Christ's temptation in the wilderness, the Lord is seen undoing the works of the Devil by the anointing of the Spirit, *"The Spirit of the Lord is upon me, because he hath anointed me to preach the Gospel to the poor; he hath sent me to heal the brokenhearted, to preach deliverance to the captives, and recovering of sight to the blind, to set at liberty them that are bruised"* (Luke 4:18).

> **How God anointed Jesus of Nazareth with the Holy Ghost and with power: who went about doing good and healing all that were oppressed of the devil; for God was with him.**
> **Acts 10:38**

The Holy Spirit was the one who gave Jesus the power to heal the sick and cast out devils, as well as raise the dead to life. The common denominator that links the three people Jesus raised from the dead is their age. They were young and had not yet fulfilled their promised long life.

Jairus said, *"My little daughter lieth at the point of death:"* (Mark 5:23). She was his little girl, just twelve years old (Mark 5:42), and death took her life. However, a hand was about to take hold of her little hand. The mother and father were watching, and Jesus spoke, and death fled, and life came.

We love our mothers. A mother who was a widow had her *"only son"* (Luke 7:12) die. Some commentators believe that the phrase "only son" could also mean only child.

When Jesus saw the funeral procession coming, he had compassion for her. *"And he came and touched the bier: and they that bare him stood still. And he said, Young man, I say unto thee, Arise. And he that was dead sat up, and began to speak"* (Luke 7:13, 14). He was a young man, and long life was his promise too.

Our third story of Jesus raising the dead was that of his friend Lazarus. A message came, *"Therefore his sisters sent unto him, saying, Lord, behold, he whom thou lovest is sick."* (John 11:3). Let me say this to encourage you just because you are sick does not mean that the Lord does not love you.

My wife and I have been to this site in the Holy Land. Where Jesus was when he received this message, and the location of Lazarus' tomb is only a little over a mile apart. Jesus stayed where he was for two days! Jesus waited for Lazarus to die. Why?

Jesus said, *"This sickness is not unto death, but for the glory of God, that the Son of God might be glorified thereby"* (John 11:4). Christ's answer here is similar to the story of the young blind man. *"Jesus answered, Neither hath this man sinned, nor his parents: but that the works of God should be made manifest in him"* (John 9:3).

Sickness and premature death does not bring God glory, but; healing from blindness and Lazarus being raised from the dead brought great glory to God's power. Jesus encouraged Martha, *"If thou wouldest believe, thou shouldest see the glory of God?"* (John 11:40).

Here then, is the reason Jesus raised the dead, *"That they may believe that thou hast sent me."* (John 11:42). Lazarus came forth and was loosed from his grave clothes.

Jesus commanded the disciples to do the same works he had done.

> **Heal the sick, cleanse the lepers, RAISE THE DEAD, cast out devils: freely ye have received, freely give.**
>
> **Matthew 10:8**

The apostle Paul raised a young man that had fallen and died.

> **And there sat in a window a certain young man named Eutychus, being fallen into a deep sleep: and as Paul was long preaching, he sunk down with sleep, and fell down from the third loft, and WAS TAKEN UP DEAD. And Paul went down, and fell on him, and embracing him said, Trouble not yourselves; for HIS LIFE IS IN HIM. When he, therefore, was come up again, and had broken bread, and eaten, and talked a long while, even till break of day, so he departed. And they brought the young man ALIVE, and were not a little comforted.**
>
> **Acts 20:7-12**

My Dad used to tell us, "Remember not to preach

too long as you don't want to kill anybody, but if you do, make sure you bring them to life."

SMITH WIGGLESWORTH RAISED HIS WIFE FROM THE DEAD

One of the books that I have treasured over the years is *Smith Wigglesworth, The Secret of His Power* by Albert Hibbert. He personally knew Wigglesworth and went to his home and fellowshipped with this great man of God. He and his family were in church the day when Wigglesworth walked in and moments later, Wigglesworth went to Heaven. His son-in-law, James Salter, announced it to those that had come to Pastor Richardson's funeral.

Albert Hibbert tells the story of Wigglesworth raising his wife from the dead.

> On New Year's Day, 1913, his beloved wife Mary Jane, whom he affectionately called "Polly," set off to fulfill a preaching engagement. During the trip, she died suddenly. The body was taken back to her home. At Brother Wigglesworth's instructions, the lifeless form of his beloved was carried to her room and laid on the bed. When the men who had brought her body left, Smith

closed the door. In the name of Jesus Christ, he rebuked death and ordered it to give her up. His wife opened her eyes and looked straight at him.

"Why have you done this, Smith?" She asked.

"Polly, I need you," he said.

"Smith, my work is finished," she answered. "God wants me."

They talked for quite some time; then Wigglesworth said, "Alright, I will let you go."

She lay back upon the pillow and went with the Lord. In such a matter so important to his happiness Wigglesworth willingly bowed to the will of God.[3]

There are three gifts that come into operation to raise the dead: the gift of faith, the working of miracles, and then the gifts of healing. We see Wigglesworth, by the gift of faith, called his wife's spirit back into her body *before* she came back. The working of miracles raises the person up, as in the story of Jairus' daughter and the widow of Nain's son. Additionally, there is the gift of healing involved that keeps that which caused the death from immediately taking the life again.

---

3. Hibbert, Albert. *Smith Wigglesworth: The Secret of His Power,* Harrison House, Tulsa, OK, 1982, pp. 26–27.

There are very few that operate in these three gifts. However, the Lord would not have told us to raise the dead unless he gave us the ability to follow his command.

3. *Supernatural Transportation*

There are three Bible examples of supernatural transportation that I would like to examine. The story of Elijah, who outran the king's horses (1 Kings 18:46). Jesus and the disciples were immediately transported to the shore (John 6:21). Philip carried bodily to Azotus (Acts 8:40).

When we look at the nine gifts of the Spirit, there are eight gifts that DO something, and one gift—the gift of faith—which RECEIVES something. There are three stories of Scripture that fall into the category of supernatural transportation that was received by God's servants.

ELIJAH OUTRUNS THE HORSES AND CHARIOT

And it came to pass in the meanwhile, that the Heaven was black with clouds and wind, and there was a great rain.

> And Ahab rode, and went to Jezreel. And the hand of the Lord was on Elijah; and he girded up his loins, and ran before Ahab to the entrance of Jezreel.
>
> **1 Kings 18:45, 46**

The anointing of the Spirit of God came upon the prophet Elijah, and he outran the horses and chariot of Ahab, and he beat them and arrived first at the entrance of Jezreel. There was a storm that was coming, but it came as a result of Elijah's prayer.

Elijah had just confronted the prophets of Baal, which Ahab and his evil wife Jezebel had allowed to operate in the nation. God sends fire down from Heaven and consumes the sacrifice on the altar. The people then turned back to God. Elijah then has these false prophets slain.

It is now that the drought is over, and Elijah prophesies, *"I hear the sound of abundance of rain."* It is when the false is removed, and the truth of God's Word is honored, then and only then will the Lord send *"times of refreshing"* from his presence. (Acts 3:19)

I believe that the Lord brought Elijah to Jezreel first to show that repentance brings blessing. Ahab's message was one of compromise, and it brought a curse. Let all present-day leadership remember God has the final say.

THE NIGHT JESUS TOOK THE WHEEL

I was preaching in eastern North Carolina. The meeting was strong, and I gave it my all. Several nights I drove back and forth to my parents' home in Tidewater. It was about an hour and forty-minute drive. The air conditioner in my car was broken, so I rolled the windows down and turned the radio up loud, fighting to stay awake.

Just before that straight stretch on 17 near the Dismal swamp, I almost fell asleep. I prayed, "Lord, speed up my journey." My head dropped, and when I snapped back to attention, I was in Suffolk! I got home, and when I walked in, my parents were still up. I had been getting back at midnight but when I looked at the clock it was 11:00 pm.

The Lord had somehow trimmed one hour off my journey!

JESUS SAVES THE DISCIPLES SUPERNATURALLY

> And the sea arose by reason of a great wind that blew. So when they had rowed about five and twenty or thirty furlongs, they saw Jesus walking on the

sea, and drawing nigh unto the ship: and they were afraid. But he saith unto them, It is I; be not afraid. Then they willingly received him into the ship: and IMMEDIATELY the ship was at the land whither they went.

         John 6:18-21

The Lord is always with us to help us. He has promised to never leave us or forsake us (Hebrews 13:5). When the storms of life are raging, he stands by us. Fear cannot overcome the child of God when the faith of God comes.

I have been on the Sea of Galilee. It is about thirteen miles long and eight miles wide. The disciples were about two to three miles out on the sea when a great storm arose. Many of these disciples were fishermen, and the fact that *"they were afraid"* shows us the intensity and fierceness of this storm.

Then here comes Jesus walking on the water! At first, they thought it was a ghost or demon spirit. Christ calls out to them, *"It is I be not afraid!"* (John 6:20). He gets in the ship, and instantly the ship is supernaturally transported to the shore! I love this story because no matter where you are, there is supernatural deliverance that removes you from the storm.

CROSSING THE RIVER

One of the books in my library is *TIMNATH-SERAH* which contains printed sermons by A. N. Trotter. He was a missionary to Africa and served to establish churches for the Assemblies of God there. Brother Trotter was related to the Garlocks, who were connected to the Apponaug church in Rhode Island, near my wife's home. My Dad served in this fellowship at about the same time and loved these men of God.

The story takes place in West Africa and stirred my faith as a young man when I heard it. Blackwater fever was sweeping that part of the continent. Brother Trotter was in the bush with several young men who carried the tents and equipment when he was attacked by the fever.

It was a long way back to the compound where he hoped to get treatment, so they started out for the mission compound. They came to a river that normally was just a shallow stream but heavy rains had swollen the river and flooded the banks.

Brother Trotter had them set up the tents, and they waited, knowing that it might be days before they could cross. His fever grew worse, and he went into his tent to rest, and he prayed Lord help us to get across the river. They all awakened the next morning, and when they came out of their tents, they were on the other bank! God supernaturally moved them and their equipment in the night!

PHILIP WAS CAUGHT UP

> And when they were come up out of the water, **THE SPIRIT OF THE LORD CAUGHT AWAY PHILIP**, that the eunuch saw him no more: and he went on his way rejoicing. But Philip was found at Azotus: and passing through he preached in all the cities, till he came to Cæsarea.
>
> **Acts 8:39, 40**

The evangelist Philip had just had a mighty revival in Samaria. The whole city was filled with joy as devils were cast out and the lame were healed. The apostles at Jerusalem heard the great story of what God was doing, and Peter and John came down and prayed for the people to receive the Holy Ghost, and they did (Acts 8:5-15).

Then an angel appeared to Philip and gave him an instruction as to where to go next (Acts 8:26). He saw an important man from Ethiopia who worked for the queen. The Spirit told him to go to the man, and he did. The man got saved, and Philip baptized him in water.

Then the Spirit caught Philip up and deposited him in Azotus. I believe that this was a literal transportation by the Spirit. It also speaks to the urgency of world evangelization and prophetically of the acceleration of getting the Gospel out in the last days. We must use every means possible to go.

MUD AND RICE

Dr. Sumrall tells the story of a preacher that dreamed every night of preaching in a village in China. He pastored a church in the eastern part of the States, but his passion was world missions.

The pastor dreamed for nights that he went to a village in China and preached to the people there. This went on for weeks, and he saw the people saved and healed. Then he would wake up in the parsonage next to his church in the States.

It seemed so real to the pastor. One morning when he awoke, he found mud and rice kernels on his slippers! He remembered walking through a rice paddy to get to the village in his dreams. Had the Lord supernaturally transported him in the night?

GOOD MORNING, VIETNAM

Bert Clendennen, a pastor from Beaumont, Texas, told me that before the Vietnam War, he had many dreams of preaching in Vietnam. He said that he would go to a village, and the people would gather to hear him preach. He related the story to me that the villagers were saved and healed and filled with the Spirit.

The day came years later that the Vietnam War began. Brother Clendennen applied to be a chaplain and was accepted by the Army. He flew to Saigon and was checking into a hotel there when a Vietnamese colonel came over to him.

"Where have you been?" Brother Clendennen turned to him and told him I just got here. The man asked him, "Have you ever been to Vietnam before?" He told him no. The colonel said, "You preached in my village years ago. I am saved and filled with the Holy Ghost because of your preaching. I have looked for you for years, and I recognized you when you just walked in."

Brother Clendennen said to me, "What if I had gone to Vietnam then, and the Lord used me for a revival that would have kept the nation from war?" Heaven knows the answer.

4. Transfer of the anointing or impartation

Ministering by the Spirit is both a privilege and a necessity. What a wonderful honor to be used by the Lord to bring to another the blessings of the Spirit of God. He gives hope to the hopeless and help to the helpless.

There is a divine order to the Spirit, and we are reminded, *"Let all things be done decently and in order"* (1 Corinthians 14:40).

There is a divine transfer of the things of the Spirit. Whether it is seen in Moses' leadership being transferred to Joshua, *"as I was with Moses so shall I be with you"* (Joshua 1:5), or let a *"double portion"* of your spirit be mine (2 Kings 2:9), the encouragement of Paul to Timothy was to *"stir up the gift"* that was in him that he had received by Paul laying his hands on him (2 Timothy 1:6).

The anointings that the Lord has placed on the Earth are to be maintained and passed on to others. This is clearly seen in the blessings that were passed down by the patriarchs.

Abraham made provision for Isaac.

Isaac laid his hands and transferred the blessing to Jacob.

Joseph received a supernatural blessing and then blessed his father again.

We are reminded that Jesus laid his hands on many, and healing came.

The apostles transferred the power of the Spirit by the laying on of hands.

We, too, have been commanded to go to the world and lay hands upon the sick and cast out devils.

It is the gift of faith that activates this supernatural anointing which is then transferred to others. The gift of faith comes upon us to see people filled with the Holy Ghost when we lay hands upon them.

> **For I long to see you, that I may IMPART unto you some spiritual gift, to the end ye may be established;**
> **Romans 1:11**

The Holy Spirit was given to us by the impartation of the Father *"And I will pray the Father, and he shall give you another Comforter, that he may abide with you forever;"* (John 14:16).

It would seem that Peter and John, as well as Paul operated in the gift of faith in imparting the Holy Spirit to believers by the laying on of hands. This was the case in Samaria when Philip had a great move of God that saw the entire city filled with the joy of the Lord.

> Now when the apostles which were at Jerusalem heard that Samaria had received the word of God, they sent unto them Peter and John: who, when they were come down, prayed for them, that they might receive the Holy Ghost: (for as yet he was fallen upon none of them: only they were baptized in the name of the Lord Jesus.) **THEN LAID THEY THEIR HANDS ON THEM, AND THEY RECEIVED THE HOLY GHOST.**
>
> Acts 8:14-17

The Apostle Paul had a similar experience when he ministered in Ephesus. He found a group of men who were disciples and sought to find out if they had received the baptism of the Holy Spirit.

Paul taught them about the different baptisms of John and then of Christ. The Bible says that they were all baptized in the name of the Lord Jesus:

> And when Paul had **LAID HIS HANDS** upon them, the Holy Ghost came on them; and they spake with tongues, and prophesied.
>
> Acts 19:6

The gift of faith then is used to transfer the anointing of the Spirit in that a special faith comes before the manifestation or administration.

The Lord has been so good to me and my family over the years. My heart's desire is to glorify his goodness and power and tell our world of his wonderful love for man. The gifts of the Spirit are given to help people succeed in life and overcome the power of the evil one.

CHAPTER 7

Questions and Answers About the Gift of Faith

When we study the gifts of the Spirit, we are reminded, *"Now concerning spiritual gifts, brethren, I would not have you ignorant"* (1 Corinthians 12:1). The Lord does not place a premium on ignorance or stupidity.

We are reminded that:

> **My people are destroyed for lack of knowledge:**
> **Hosea 4:6**

There are some questions that many have about the gifts of the Spirit and the gift of faith in particular. Although we cannot answer every question, I do believe that the Word of God contains the answers that we are looking for.

There are two verses that help us to receive understanding:

> **STUDY to shew thyself approved unto God, a workman that needeth not to be ashamed, rightly dividing the word of truth.**
>
> **2 Timothy 2:15**

> **But sanctify the Lord God in your hearts: and be ready always to give an ANSWER to every man that asketh you a reason of the hope that is in you with meekness and fear:**
>
> **1 Peter 3:15**

Let us examine a few of the questions that people have asked about the gifts of the Spirit and, in particular, the gift of faith.

QUESTION: HOW DO THE GIFTS OF THE SPIRIT WORK, AND WHY?

All of the gifts of the Spirit and their operation and ministry are a manifestation of the Holy Spirit at work.

> But the MANIFESTATION of the Spirit is given to every man to profit withal.
>
> 1 Corinthians 12:7

Strong's Concordance translates the word *"manifestation"* (G5319) as *"a shining forth;"* (visible, manifest, evident or apparent, bringing light). The gifts of the Spirit then are a light-based projection of the working of the Spirit of God. When any of the nine gifts are in operation at that moment, there is a radiant light of God's presence and glory.

The *power gifts* release his POWER.
The *utterance gifts* release his PRESENCE.
The *revelation gifts* release his PURPOSE.

> The entrance of thy words giveth LIGHT; it giveth understanding unto the simple.
>
> Psalm 119:130

The gifts of the Spirit only work in connection to the Word of God. They should always be seen as a confirmation of that Word.

> And they went forth, and preached everywhere, the Lord working with them,

and confirming the word with signs following. Amen.
>Mark 16:20

The Spirit of the Lord is the power of God working upon the earth to do the Father's will.

QUESTION: WHY DO I BELIEVE THE GIFT OF FAITH WILL INCREASE IN OPERATION IN THESE END-TIMES?

It is impossible for the evil that is in the world to become greater than the anointing in you! *"Because greater is he that is in you, than he that is in the world."* (1 John 4:4). The Scriptures reveal that evil will increase in the last days.

> But evil men and seducers shall wax
> WORSE and WORSE, deceiving,
> and being deceived.
> 2 Timothy 3:13

Paul prophesied in his second letter to Timothy, *"This know also, that IN THE LAST DAYS perilous times shall come"* (2 Timothy 3:1).

Jesus warned us of these days of peril as he talked

to his disciples on the Mount of Olives. He called this time the *"beginning of sorrows"* (Matthew 24:8). The gift of faith is activated by danger (peril) and need.

The gift of faith is the Holy Spirit's immediate response to peril and dangerous attacks of the enemy. The shield of faith (Ephesians 6:16) would be a symbol of the gift of faith. It cuts off every attack of the enemy. This gift *"quenches all"* those fiery darts of the enemy that come against you.

No weapon shall succeed against the child of God (Isaiah 54:17). Prophetically and biblically, the anointing of the Holy Spirit and his gifts will always be greater in manifestation than any evil work of the devil.

QUESTION: HOW DOES THE GIFT OF FAITH WORK, AND DOES IT EVER FAIL?

The gift of faith is the ability given by the Spirit to the believer to receive the faith of God in the present moment for supernatural provision and protection. It is God in you, believing through you and for you.

Weymouth, in his commentary, calls it *"special faith."* *The Amplified Bible* refers to it as *[wonder-working faith]*.

It would seem to be activated by an immediate crisis or danger.

If the gift of faith could fail, then the Holy Spirit

would have to fail. Daniel would have been eaten by the lions, the three Hebrew boys would have burnt up, and Jonah would have drowned with the whale.

A believer may not fully yield to the Spirit or may allow certain things in his or her life that hinder the gift of faith from working (Romans 6:13), or if you are double-minded, then you cannot *receive* from the Lord. (James 1:6-8). The gift of faith *receives*. God cannot fail!

QUESTION: CAN A SINNER OPERATE IN THE GIFTS?

The answer is no. Then we must ask the question about the manifestations of the Spirit in relationship to those who live in hypocrisy and apostasy.

> **For the gifts and calling of God are without repentance.** **Romans 11:29**

This would seem to indicate that a backslidden man or woman could operate in the gifts. There are those who were once called and anointed that have backslidden and seemingly continue in ministry.

So we see the difference between a sinner who has not yet received the Holy Spirit and a believer who has received Christ and been filled with the Spirit as two different conditions of the soul. Concerning the latter group of those who at one time were saved and on fire for God, we read the following Scripture:

> **For it is impossible for those who were once enlightened, and have tasted of the heavenly gift, and were made partakers of the Holy Ghost, And have tasted the good word of God, and the powers of the world to come, If they shall fall away, to renew them again unto repentance; seeing they crucify to themselves the Son of God afresh, and put him to an open shame.**
> **Hebrews 6:4-6**

God always honors His Word to the people who believe His Word, even when the minister is not living for God which is why we should keep our eyes upon Jesus.

I do believe that there are *"counterfeits"* to the gifts. However, that only means there are the real gifts of the Holy Spirit. When I was in Haiti I watched voodoo priests lay hands on people who fell upon the ground while the voodoo drums played. They were not slain by the Spirit of God, but this ritual released evil spirits. Whereas our worship brings the presence of God, and no one can stop our praise! Jesus said:

> **For there shall arise false Christs, and false prophets, and shall shew great signs and wonders; insomuch that, if it were possible, they shall deceive the very elect.**
> **Matthew 24:24**

The anti-Christ will operate:

> **after the working of Satan with all power and signs and lying wonders,**
> **2 Thessalonians 2:9**

These are false gifts and signs and wonders which never operate in the redemptive context. The devil cannot redeem a soul from sin. He cannot heal sicknesses or diseases.

QUESTION: ARE THE GIFTS, SUCH AS TONGUES AND MIRACLES, DEMONS AT WORK?

> **Many will say to me in that day, Lord, Lord, have we not prophesied in thy name? and in thy name have cast out**

> devils? and in thy name done many wonderful works? And then will I profess unto them, I never knew you: depart from me, ye that work iniquity.
>
> Matthew 7:22, 23

They appealed to the works of what God did through them in prophesying and casting out devils and the working of miracles. Jesus points to their lifestyle of iniquity, which disqualified them from Heaven.

If, as some claim, that the ministry of healing and the other gifts of the Spirit are done by the devil, then what would you say about the ministry of Jesus, the apostles, and the ministry of Paul? Are you saying that they operated by Satan's power?

Jesus dealt with this same religious spirit in his day. The scribes came down from Jerusalem they accused Jesus of casting out devils by Satan's power. Jesus answered them;

> How can Satan cast out Satan? And if a kingdom be divided against itself, that kingdom cannot stand. And if a house be divided against itself, that house cannot stand.
>
> Mark 3:23-25

Can the devil heal? If there was a time the devil could heal, then why did Jesus appeal to his working of miracles as evidential proof that he was God's Son?

> **When the men were come unto him, they said, John Baptist hath sent us unto thee, saying, ART THOU HE THAT SHOULD COME or look we for another? And in that same hour he cured many of their infirmities and plagues, and of evil spirits; and unto many that were blind he gave sight. Then Jesus answering said unto them, Go your way, and TELL JOHN what things ye have seen and heard; how that THE BLIND SEE, THE LAME WALK, THE LEPERS ARE CLEANSED, THE DEAF HEAR, THE DEAD ARE RAISED, TO THE POOR THE GOSPEL IS PREACHED. And blessed is he, whosoever shall not be offended in me.**
>
> Luke 7:20-23

The message Jesus sent to John the Baptist was these miracles which you have seen and heard attest to the fact that I am he.

QUESTION: WHAT IS A "POINT OF CONTACT," AND ARE THERE ANY OTHER BIBLE EXAMPLES OF THE GIFT OF FAITH RELATED TO THEIR USE?

God has used natural means to bring supernatural results. The gift of faith is the link between these two worlds. When Hezekiah was sick unto death, the Lord sent Isaiah to tell him to set his house in order for he would die. The king turned his face to the wall and prayed, and God added years to his life.

The Lord told Isaiah to go back and give this instruction:

> **Let them take a lump of figs, and lay it for a plaister upon the boil, and he shall recover.**
> **Isaiah 38:21**

Why a lump of figs for healing? (Isaiah 38:21). Isaiah received *knowledge* from the Lord regarding what to do before Hezekiah recovered. The figs were a *"point of contact,"* which is the gift of faith working *before* the gifts of healing.

Why did Moses use a tree and cast it upon the bitter waters for them to be healed? Moses received knowledge about what to do before the waters were healed.

That is the gift of faith (Exodus 15:25). The water was bitter. This produced a crisis, and the Lord gave them *supernatural provision* at that moment.

Why did Gideon use a fleece to receive a word from the Lord? (Judges 6:36-40). The fleece was a *"point of contact"* to receive the enablement from the Lord to bring about the defeat of the enemy. That was a part of the gift of faith Gideon operated in.

Why did Elisha tell Naaman to dip in the *muddy water* to be healed of leprosy? (2 Kings 5:10). Elisha knew at that moment that the muddy stream was Naaman's *"point of contact."*

Why did a woman know to touch the *hem of Jesus' garment* to be healed? (Mark 5:28, 29). That garment became the *"point of contact"* for her.

How did the people know that *Peter's shadow* would bring healing to the sick as he walked by? *"Insomuch that they brought forth the sick into the streets, and laid them on beds and couches, that at the least the shadow of Peter passing by might overshadow some of them."* (Acts 5:15). The shadow did not heal, but it was who was in the shadow. Here the gift of faith blessed the masses.

Why did Jesus spit upon the ground and mix it with the clay to anoint the eyes of the young blind man? *"When he had thus spoken, he spat on the ground, and made clay of the spittle, and he anointed the eyes of the blind man with the clay, and said unto him, Go, wash in the pool of Siloam, (which is by interpretation, Sent.) He went his way therefore, and washed, and came seeing"* (John 9:6, 7). The spit mixed with the clay became the young blind man's *"point of contact."* The miracle took place after this.

I have learned that these scriptural examples are *"a point of contact"* prompted at these moments by the gift of faith.

QUESTION: HOW DID PAUL KNOW TO USE HANDKERCHIEFS AND APRONS FOR SPECIAL MIRACLES?

And God wrought SPECIAL MIRACLES by the hands of Paul:
Acts 19:11

The gift of faith is called *"special faith"* in Weymouth's translation. Then we read that God worked *"special miracles"* (Acts 19:11, 12) through Paul's ministry. Since each gift operates independently, then Paul received *"special faith"* before the handkerchiefs and aprons were sent out, producing *"special miracles."*

There is no healing power in cloth itself. Everyone that is wearing clothes would be healed if that were so. It was what got into the cloth that produced the miracles of diseases being healed and devils being cast out.

The gift of faith produces a *knowing* at the moment of crisis, which *receives* the breakthrough for the miracle that is needed. What was in the mind of Paul? How did he know to do this, and why did this knowledge produce these *special miracles?*

> **But unto you that fear my name shall the Sun of righteousness arise with HEALING IN HIS WINGS; and ye shall go forth, and grow up as calves of the stall.**
> **Malachi 4:2**

In *Strong's Concordance*, the word for wings is "*kanaph.*" It means rays of light, and it is also used as a literal reference to a skirt or a border of a garment. Many Bible scholars agree that (Malachi 4:2) is a reference to the coming Messiah, who is Christ.

Certainly, Paul knew this teaching of the prophet Malachi. Perhaps, he knew the story of the woman with the issue of blood (Mark 5:25-34). The Bible records that she touched Christ's clothes (Mark 5:28). When she did, the plague she suffered with was healed! One of the things that this story reveals is the power of God is released by a *"point of contact."*

QUESTION: HOW DID THE LORD TEACH ME TO OPERATE BY THE GIFT OF FAITH IN THE USE OF A "POINT OF CONTACT?"

The Lord first taught me about the use of a *"point of contact"* in Kingston, Jamaica, in 1975. I was holding a soul-winning crusade in the Red Hills, at 52 Mannings Hill Road, on a large parking lot of a church.

Night after night, the Lord was performing wonderful miracles, and the people were coming from far and near. We had advertised in Kingston's *Daily Gleaner* newspaper, but the miracles were the better advertisement, and the crowds grew each night.

One night, a woman came up to me and asked me for my handkerchief. I asked her why she would want my damp handkerchief. I had been using it all night to mop my wet brow. It was hot and muggy on that Caribbean island.

She told me she wanted to take it home to her crippled mother so she would be healed. When she told me that, I told her, "I don't believe in gimmicks." The Lord used that little Jamaican woman to change my mind. "IT'S IN THE BIBLE, PREACHER MAN!"

She then quoted Acts 19:11, 12. *"And God wrought special miracles by the hands of Paul: so that from his body were brought unto the sick handkerchiefs or aprons, and the dis-*

eases departed from them, and the evil spirits went out of them."

I handed her my handkerchief.

The next night, as I headed to the platform, an older woman stopped me and said, "Here is your handkerchief." I knew that this was not the young lady that I had given it to the night before. When suddenly, out of the dark, came the young woman I had given it to. She said, "Here is my mother, and the Lord healed her!"

Her mother had been crippled for many years and could not come to the meeting. Her daughter believed what the Bible said about the handkerchiefs Paul used and wanted mine for her mother's healing.

When she went home the night before, she placed it on her mother, who was sleeping in the bed. "This morning, when I woke up, I heard someone sweeping on my patio. When I looked out, it was my mother freely walking for the first time in years."

Since that time, I have prayed over and sent out tens of thousands of these anointed cloths freely without charge. The testimonies have been amazing. That woman was healed by the power of God through a *"point of contact."*

QUESTION: WHAT IS IT THAT THE GIFT OF FAITH RELEASES?

Faith is the nature of God. Since God, who is eternal, remains in his holy habitation (Psalm 33:14) and never changes in his nature (Malachi 3:6), then there is a tangible substance in the anointing that remains.

> **Now faith is the SUBSTANCE of things hoped for, the evidence of things not seen.**
> **Hebrews 11:1**

The anointing is the Spirit's ability, capacity, and force to accomplish the Lord's purposes for his great plan. How we love the anointing. That anointing refreshes, renews, reactivates you, and breaks off and destroys the working of the enemy against you.

> **But the anointing which ye have received of him ABIDETH in you,**
> **1 John 2:27**

Therefore the tangible substance of the anointing gets in your spirit and remains in your body. There is an interesting story that illustrates this truth.

> And it came to pass, as they were burying a man, that, behold, they spied a band of men; and they cast the man into the sepulchre of Elisha: and when the man was let down, and touched THE BONES of Elisha, he revived, and stood up on his feet.
>
> 2 Kings 13:21

Elisha was an Old Testament prophet who had a strong desire for the anointing of the Spirit of God. We are introduced to him when God instructed Elijah to anoint him to be a prophet (1 Kings 19:16).

Understand that although he was called to be a prophet, he still had to pass the test of accountability to be chosen as the successor to Elijah. *"For many are called, but few are chosen"* (Matthew 22:14).

When it was time for Elijah to go to Heaven, Elisha journeyed with him. Elisha's desire is seen in his refusal to stay behind (2 Kings 2:1-14).

During his ministry, God performed eight miracles through Elijah. Elisha's prayer was, *"I pray thee, let a double portion of thy spirit be upon me"* (2 Kings 2:9).

The day that Elisha died he had seen only fifteen miracles take place in his ministry, one short of sixteen. Remember, every time the Lord used him, that tangible anointing was abiding in his spirit and bones.

The sixteenth miracle took place after Elisha was dead and buried. A soldier killed on the field of battle is lowered down onto the grave of Elisha. When he touched Elisha's bones, he revived and came alive.

I believe the more you operate in the gifts, the more skilled you become in their administration. That tangible anointing builds up in your spirit, soul, and body. That tangible anointing never leaves you.

QUESTION: DOES THE GIFT OF FAITH OPERATE FOR PROPERTY AND LANDS AND THE RECEIVING OF MONEY?

I immediately thought of when the Lord gave me three houses in Norfolk, Virginia. A lawyer had given me an office for my ministry in his law complex. One day Barry came to me and said there was a client that would like to leave some of her property to a ministry.

He had helped me get incorporated and was on the ministry board of directors. I received this free gift of properties and sold them to buy some of my first crusade equipment for the ministry.

I just had been listening to a recorded message by R.W. Schambach on how God gave him the Young Women's - Young Men's Hebrew Association building on Martin Luther King Boulevard, a building, and property in Newark, New Jersey.

One night after church, the Lord told him to walk around the building, and he would give it to him. Brother Schambach tells how he marched around that building like Joshua and the children of Israel walked around Jericho (Joshua 6:1-20).

The next day, someone put a for sale sign on the front of the property. Brother Schambach took it out and went down to the realtor's office, Feaster and Feaster. He jokingly said, "Two Irish brothers."

The realtor asked him what he was doing with the sign. He had just put it there that morning. Brother Schambach told him that the property was his. The realtor told him it was owned by an insurance company in North Carolina. "Call them," he told the realtor.

Brother Schambach slapped a five-dollar bill down on the realtor's desk. The man picked up the phone and called the offices. The call did not go through the switchboard but rang directly into the board room where they were meeting that morning.

The realtor spoke with the president of the company. "I have got a crazy preacher here in my office, and he wants to buy your building" He turned around and asked Brother Schambach, "How much will you offer?"

Brother Schambach bowed his head, and the Holy Spirit gave him a figure; it was $50,000. The realtor scoffed at him and said it was worth hundreds of thousands. "Just tell them," Schambach said.

Reluctantly the realtor told the president and started saying, "Yes, sir, I understand. No, sir. Alright, I will," and hung up. He turned to Brother Schambach and said, "You're not so crazy after all."

The insurance company had a banner year in sales. The president told the realtor to give it to him for the $50,000, and they would write the difference off. Newark Miracle Temple was launched, and I had the privilege to preach there in the 1980s.

Abraham received the land of Promise (Hebrews 11:8-10).

Caleb received a mountain (Joshua 14:12, 13).

Joshua received Timnath-Serah (Joshua 19:50).

Peter received miracle money (Matthew 17:27).

The gift of faith is a part of God's unlimited ability or power given at the moment of need to the believer to achieve what the Lord wants to be done through the life of that one.

Suddenly you know on the inside, "That is my property; that is my building. My money will come in, and I will make it." The gift of faith places you in a position to receive in times of trouble and give supernatural provision.

The gift of faith says you're going to make it!

QUESTION: HOW DOES THE GIFT OF FAITH BRING PEACE?

The gift of faith overcomes demonic plans of confusion by bringing an alignment to the will of God for your life.

> **For God is not the author of confusion, but of PEACE, as it is in all churches of the saints.**
> **1 Corinthians 14:33**

It is not a feeling. It is more of a knowing. It produces peace and calm in the midst of turmoil and challenge. It provides courage in the time of crisis.

It is Daniel enjoying peace and safety in the lion's den.

It is the Hebrew children walking peacefully in the fiery furnace.

It is Paul praying peacefully in the great storm — Euroclydon.

It is Elijah resting peacefully at the brook Cherith.

It is Paul and Silas singing and praising God at midnight in the prison.

It is Job's confession in the time of his affliction.

It is Esther in the King's court.

It is Peter's act of going and finding a coin in the fish's mouth.

It is Jesus feeding the 5,000.

It is released by the Holy Spirit's ministry.

It is God revealing Himself at the point of our receiving.

The gift of faith makes the impossible possible!

THE GIFT OF FAITH HAS SUSTAINED ME

My wife and I traveled for eight years without a home or an apartment. When we were off, we would stay with our parents. Her parents were in New England, and if our ministry was there and we had time off, we would stay with them.

My parents lived in Virginia. We traveled out of there to some of the southern states. One year, we spent Christmas and the New Year with my parents. I had no invitations and no money. My Dad and Mom were headed to California to preach, and Dad left me to take care of the house.

One day, Bonnie said, "This is the last of the food." She had taken some ground beef and made a meatloaf out of it. The refrigerator was empty. My wallet was empty. She put water in a ketchup bottle to get the last of it out. It was on top of the smallest meatloaf I ever saw. It shrank while she cooked it.

I bowed my head to pray. Something big exploded in my spirit. I prayed as if I had all the food I needed. I prayed as if my bank account was full. I believe the Lord gave my wife and me an operation of the gift of faith that day.

The phone rang! I knew in my spirit who it was and that he was going to give us $1,000. When I answered, I called him by name. There was no Caller ID in those days, and he said, "Did my wife tell you I was going to call?"

I cut him off and said, "Look, I need the money now before the bank closes." He told me that he wondered how I knew he had money for us. Then I said, "It is $1,000." The phone line went quiet. Then he said, "I do, and I will meet you down at the plaza."

We met in the parking lot, and I ran and got the check and thanked him and jumped in my car and went to the bank drive-thru, and cashed the check. The next stop was the Food Lion grocery store.

I ran in and grabbed two carts. One was filled with steaks, chickens, hams, lunch meat, and cheeses. The other I filled with vegetables, fruit, eggs, bread, milk, and anything that I could get.

Then I went across the street and filled my car with gas. My Dad heated the home with kerosene, so I filled two ten-gallon containers. When I got home, my wife and I praised God for his great care. She made a feast!

I gave my tithe at church on Sunday. We paid our car payment and insurance. We had money left over. That was a great moment of knowing we had received, in our most desperate circumstance, supernatural help and provision.

LAST WORDS

I have fasted and prayed over these studies early in the mornings and late in the nights. My God is real. He has kept and protected me. I have been filled with his Spirit. I have failed him, but he has never failed me.

There are churches to be built and Bible schools to be filled. There are missions to be accomplished in the nations. There are Evangelists to be supported for soul-winning crusades. There are television networks that need to be strengthened and new ones built. The Gospel must go forward!

My last words of encouragement to you are that the gift of faith is available to you today. God has a great work for you to do. I have prayed over these books like an anointed prayer cloth so that you will receive the gift of faith.

DOWNLOAD OUR APP.

Search "Ted Shuttlesworth" in the Apple App Store or the Google Play Store.

DO YOU NEED PRAYER?

Call us today: 1-888-323-2484

Visit us online: www.tedshuttlesworth.com

THE CAMELS ARE COMING

Your success in life is birthed out of your understanding of Spiritual Gifts. Their importance is critical in the end times as we deal with deception and evil.

This book is an examination of the existence and purpose of the Gifts of the Spirit. There are three Gifts that can bring a life-changing word from God. There are three Gifts that can bring healing and help for the spirit, soul, and body. There are three gifts that can reveal God's design and plan past, present, and future.

shop.tedshuttlesworth.com

WHAT I'VE LEARNED ABOUT THE BLESSING

God's blessing will take you from financial failure to a good life. Throughout the years, I have proven that the biblical principles of increase work.

I gave God one dollar when I was eighteen, and He gave me a ministry to touch the world. I have learned that The Blessing is greater than the curse and that the Lord cannot fail.

You can be the one that changes your family's financial future. Many of God's children are living far below their potential. When you understand the connection between prosperity and the winning of lost souls and faithfully operate in these biblical principles, you can expect to receive God's blessing. Each chapter contains a key that will unlock THE BLESSING and release God's best in your life.

shop.tedshuttlesworth.com

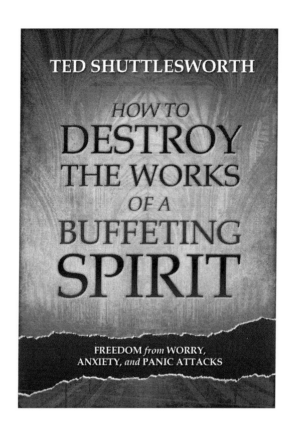

HOW TO DESTROY THE WORKS OF A BUFFETING SPIRIT

Today we are witnessing unrest and trouble which are affecting the nations of the world. There are many who are fearful because of the uncertainty of the times.

Anxiety disorders are the most common mental illness in the United States affecting 40 million adults 18 years of age and older according to the National Institute of Mental Health.

There are many people who are managing anxiety with medications, psychiatrists, and even hypnosis. What if these attacks were being caused by demon spirits? Learn what the Bible has to say about how to be free from worry, fear, anxiety, and panic attacks!

shop.tedshuttlesworth.com

HOW TO RECEIVE YOUR HEALING

It is God's will for you to be healed. Faith for healing comes from the hearing of God's Word.

"But so much the more went there a fame abroad of him: and great multitudes came together to hear, and to be healed by him of their infirmities." **Luke 5:15**

Here is a step-by-step, scriptural plan that will help you to receive your personal healing from Jesus Christ. A great faith-building book for those who have been chronically ill.

shop.tedshuttlesworth.com

Made in the USA
Monee, IL
23 June 2024

cb9d3396-adff-490d-b69b-3cc93141486dR01